Secrets of the Successful Student

Secrets of the Successful Student

Gordon D. Stein

With Cover & Drawings
by
Peter M. Herman
a.k.a. Carbo
of the
Flying Caborski Brothers

CULTURE CONCEPTS INC.
"books for learning"™

5 Darlingbrook Cres.
Toronto, Ontario
M9A 3H4 Canada

"books that won't stay on the shelf"™
1991

Secrets of the Successful Student

by

CULTURE CONCEPTS INC.
"books for learning"™

5 DARLINGBROOK CRESCENT
TORONTO, ONTARIO
M9A 3H4 CANADA

Canadian Cataloguing in Publication Data

Stein, Gordon D. (Gordon David), 1961–
Secrets of the Successful Student

ISBN 0-921472-18-8

1. College student orientation. I. Title.

LB2343.3.S74 1991 378.1'98 C91-09422-0

Typesetting: Jaytype Inc.
Drawings and Cover: ©Peter M. Herman, a.k.a. Carbo
Printed and Bound in Canada by Hearn/Kelly Printing

About the Author

Gord Stein won the Proctor & Gamble Engineering Award during his degree in Mechanical Engineering at the University of Western Ontario, Deans List during his Master of Business Adminstration at the University of Toronto and successfully completed the Canadian Securities Course.

But it was a 20% midterm in first year engineering that spurred his interest in just what it takes to be a successful student, and in helping other students to make it through.

Gord has enjoyed a successful career in Sales and Marketing with IBM Canada Ltd. and is currently President of Saber Consultants Ltd. in Toronto.

Acknowledgements

Thanks to all those who helped me to let out The Secrets. Especially my illustrator, 'Carbo' Caborski, Karisa Ambury, Cindy Faber, Cheryl Watson, Mark Kindrachuk and his personal computer, as well as a superb editor at Culture Concepts.

And most of all, thanks to my wife Ingrid who smiled reassuringly through hundreds of whaddyathinks.

Dedication

To my mother, who made me a writer
and to my wife who made me write.

Contents

Introduction

Looking for a student study guide filled with useful formulae, handy mathematical tables, summaries of the great works of literature and some speed reading tips?

Keep looking.

On to the real stuff of college life. How do you find a decent place to live? How to make sure that you don't run out of money three months into the year? How do you get a date to the formal? What is an essay and how do you create one? How do you get the sink unplugged and of course, how do you write a good exam? By the way, how about some student chow that anyone can cook quickly and on the cheap?

Welcome to ***Secrets of the Successful Student****, a stick of dynamite that will propel you through the world of higher learning and blast you out the other side as a graduate with great marks, a full social calendar and a balanced cheque book. Along the way, you'll learn to cook some Lemon, Lime and Lager Chicken, find out where the best places are to spark a new romance and how to control the mice in your apartment.*

Never before has it all been laid out so clearly for the new student, referenced so succinctly for the currently enrolled or has such a brisk stroll been provided down memory lane for the paunchy, greying sophomore of yesteryear.

Everything that you'll need to get through school is in these pages. Except of course, a chapter on cleaning.

After all, we're students aren't we?

Gord Stein

1 EXAMINING THE STUDENT BODY

– steps to dynamic dating

It had been over three months since your last date. All the bad signs were there. Some 'helpful' friends had assembled a support group for you. Hours of slightly biased personal scrutiny in the mirror had failed to yield any clues as to the reasons for your celibate existence. Even your parents had begun to offer their oh-so-current techniques to help you secure a date. The situation had grown desperate.

Like a cruise missile, friend's conversations seemed to be precisely guided – to your failures in dating. An impromptu gathering over a few drinks quickly turned to an unrequested brain storming session.

"How about Sue?" offered Mark.

"Too smart – she'd have him figured out in a second", quipped Greg, before you could offer your acceptance of the idea.

"We need someone who could relate to a dull guy. Someone not too focused on looks," suggested Ken.

"No woman is that desperate," shot back Mark, intent on dousing the last remaining flicker of your ego.

"False advertising," offered Greg to a roomful of blank stares including yours.

"False advertising. We'll run an ad in the personal column of the student paper. We'll build him up a bit. By the time she figures out what she's really in for, they'll be on a date. Mission accomplished." Greg sat back with a look of satisfaction having delivered his plum idea.

"You guys are going to advertise me?" you ask.

"OK, let's do it", came the group response to what was meant as rhetoric question.

The gang promised to get back to you with the final copy before placing the ad in the newspaper. Two days later, you catch up with Mark on campus. He flashes a big grin before passing you the typed final copy:

> *Tall, intellectual yet sensitive and conshientious guy, 21, with broad shoulders, wing tips, button downs and Polo After Shave seeks fun loving gal, 20-25 with sports car and trust fund to share quiet evenings, art gallery viewings, philosophical discussions and Nietzsche readings. Reply Box 125.*

"Nietzsche readings? Who the hell is he?" you ask in disbelief.

"Don't worry, it's intellectual stuff. Chicks dig it," assured Mark, perhaps your least trustworthy friend.

"You spelled conscientious wrong."

"Women love to correct men, they need to find something to change."

"What's this about a trust fund?"

"Read the newspaper, man. Cash is king in the 90's. You don't want a girl with equities. Too risky. The market could collapse. You'd be left with nothing. Best to be up front with these things. Trust me. "

"OK, OK. But when did I become sensitive?"

"Think sales, sometimes you have to stretch things a bit to get the order. By the way, the ad was forty six bucks. Any chance you can pay me back by Monday? Stick a cheque in my locker. Gotta run-"

"Well, I think we will need to tone it down a – forty six bucks? Don't tell me you've sent it in?"

"Of course, had to get it in quickly before all the best girls are gone. Time kills all dates. Gotta run."

Mark dashed off into the sea of knapsacks, students and bicycles. Oh boy, you think as you ponder the prospects of sifting through dozens of letters written by rich, sensitive, Polo sniffing, Nietzsche reading girls desperate to meet Mr. Conshientious.

As the days went on, you wondered how your buddies could get so excited about such nonsense. Talk about childish pursuits. Imagine actually dating someone from a personal ad. What kind of a loser would entrust the quality of their romances to the whims of the great unwashed masses who would place a personal ad? What kind of friends would subject a guy to this kind of social roulette?

Unable to stand it, your outer, carefree veneer removed, you raced down to the student paper offices and sheepishly quoted your box number.

"So you're Box 125", barked out the clerk to the assembled crowd, "You only got one response to your personal ad", she giggled.

Red faced, you snatch the envelope from her hands and storm past the delighted crowd. Finding a secluded park bench, you carefully study the envelope.

A rich parchment paper with your box number typed on the front. You quickly scan around the park before sniffing the envelope for perfume. Maybe she wears Lady Polo.

Nope, no scent.

You wonder what kind of woman lurks behind the envelope. Perhaps tall and exotic looking with a biting wit, someone you could curl up with and watch NFL games. Maybe a short pert blonde, an intellectual type who could help with your essays.

With great trepidation you begin to tear open the envelope. Whoa, maybe a saucy redhead with...

"Dear Box 125", the letter began, "I enjoyed reading your ad in the paper. Sounds like you possess some interesting qualities..."

You can't believe that anyone would find the qualities in that ad interesting.

"... While I am afraid that I can't help you with your dating problems, I am a great fan of the works of Mr. Nietzsche. I have a number of his earlier volumes and I am looking for one or two books to complete my set. If you would be interested in making some trades, please let me know. Good luck with your ad, if you get too busy and have some extra replies that you can't handle, let me know. Hope to talk to you soon. Sincerely, Jason Roberts (426) 929-3427.

"Extra replies. Lady Polo. Trust fund", you grumble, trudging back to campus.

Steps to Dynamic Dating

This chapter is divided into three sections. The first offers some juicy nuggets for you guys out there on how to attract a really steamy babe (never call 'em babes), the second part of the chapter (written mostly by my wife) offers tips for you female types to land the cash-laden teddy bear of your dreams (never call 'em teddy bears) and then the third part offers some ideas on how to impress your new catch on a student budget. While this whole thing is built for as broad an audience as possible, these days it just isn't easy. The ideas in here should be suitable for most of you. If you aren't a big dater, re-read the chapter on studying for exams.

Part One – Where to Find the Chicks

Naturally, to the get the whole process working, you will need to position yourself in the areas where women tend to congregate. Remember too, that these same women will be assessing your character by what you were doing in the place that they met you. Herewith, a list of potential hot spots, the type of chicks typically available there and the impression you make by hanging around.

The Laundromat

Cool. Set yourself up as the independent type. No mama's boy here. Get a small box of Tide (big boxes reek of economy) and some unscented Bounce sheets for the dryer. Black T shirt, faded jeans. Vintage Nicholson. A touch sensitive, but with a hint of danger. They'll love you. Bring a magazine to read, adds to the nonchalant look. Something trendy and ideally, foreign or intellectual. Try Vanity Fair, Paris Match or Architectural Digest. You want them to head back to the dorm and coo about your complexity to their roommates.

Now here's the key. A touch of helplessness. Women can't stand to see whites going in with colours. Leave out the fabric softener and they will be all over you. Dial in the wrong temperature rinse and you'll work them up to a frenzy.

When they finally rush over to help, hit them with an intense stare. Try a little Tom Cruise from Top Gun or Paul Newman from Cool Hand Luke. Beautiful.

The Gymnasium

Well rounded. Self Assured. Scope out a few of the aerobics classes to find the ones requiring minimal coordination with the hottest selection of babes (oops). Memorize a few of the moves and practice up ahead of time at home so that you can appear natural. Head back to the gym practised up and ready to go. Slide into a spot on the floor next to the woman of your dreams. Try to appear reasonably fluid, but be careful not to be too good.

By doing lunges in the opposite direction to your prospective wife, you will be able to get some eye contact going. Work through the moves and pretend to enjoy the music. However nubile and sinewy the crowd, don't stare. As the class applauds itself, saunter over and ask if you can buy her a mineral water and some carrot sticks. Dynamite.

The Car Repair Shop

Like men, women need to get their cars fixed too. Often they will be in a sullen mood, awaiting an exorbitant bill to change some greasy car part that evidently is holding them up from going about their business.

Naturally, you can tune your audience by selecting the type of repair shop to hang out at. Check your bank balance (where applicable) and head to the dealership that fixes cars least resembling the state of your account. Listen in when she speaks with the mechanic to catch a bit of the terminology. Leaving your four-hour-old BMW key fob hanging from your sweaty palm, approach the coachless lass and deliver your line.

"Control Pressure Regulator gone? Darn Bimmers. I make a great Bluefish Fettucini. How about dinner next week?"

The only person in the world sensitive to her problems has just asked her out to dinner. Don't forget your Haute Cuisine recipes. Bon Appétit.

The Cafeteria

The salad bar. Perfect. Attracts the healthy ones. Do a first pass to memorize the lay out. By sucking in your gut and cruising the salad bar you're likely to look like one of those impossibly healthy types that she's been reading about in Cosmo. Think William Hurt or Kevin Costner. (Try borrowing some of those serious round wire-frame glasses from someone).

Position yourself just upstream of that vegetarian vision and wait until her plate is about ⅔ full. Carefully select a ripe leaf of endive and artistically drape it over her tofu.

As your tongs retreat, stare deeply into her eyes and offer, "Tough to get a decent salad around here. Sorry to burden you with my endive. It just looked right on your plate. I have a class at 1:00, but I can spend a few minutes with you. My table is just over here..."

The Library

Yes, women feign studying just as much as guys. Excellent spot to zero in on some of the artsie types. Superb female density around exam time. Find that beautiful bookworm and scan a few of the titles that she is reading. Ideally, try to pick out the Dewey Decimal numbers. Head to that section of the library and grab two or three that are within about twenty feet of the books that she is reading.

Head back to her table and hang your jacket across the back of a chair. As she looks up, get a quick read on her interest level. High degree of annoyance? Pivot on your heel and re-start the procedure somewhere else. Some level of interest? Sit down and do a bit of reading. On the back of a bookmark scribble something about how the beer is warm at the campus pub and you can't concentrate ever since she sat at *your* table. Remember – home by 11. Its a school night.

PART TWO – WHERE TO FIND THE HUNKS

Face it girls, school is the place to track down those elusive Charles Bronson substitutes. By carefully manoeuvring in their habitats, you will be able to woo in the best of them. Use some caution when working in their turf, guys carry a fine line between women who are too fragile (unwilling to toss around a football on the beach) or too butch (popping off beer caps with their teeth). The other approach is to catch them where they are a little off guard. Here are a few places to start...

Big Screen Sports Bars

Check and see if there is one of these bars on campus. Scan the TV listings to find out which sports events are telecast during the week (although Monday Night Football is still a staple). If you aren't up on the sport being televised, do a little reading up or get your Dad or brother to explain it to you. If they ask pressing questions about your sudden interest in football, give them one of those 'pull-eeeezze' stares and a flick of your pony tail.

With a little knowledge (being a dangerous thing and all) under your belt, head into the bar with a girlfriend and take a position halfway between the screen and the table of your choice. Order a round of beers for yourselves, but do get glasses. Butch ain't in.

Toss out the odd carefully chosen comment about the game but don't cheer unless you are certain. Use 'uniform' rather than 'outfit', 'touchdown' rather than 'home run' and focus on the athletic accomplishments of the teams rather than the form of their anatomy. At a commercial, casually glance over at the guy who will one day weed your lawn and ask if the score has been flashed on the Cincinnati game. Touchdown.

The Grocery Store

Aha. There he is, just past the bok choy, squeezing the cantaloupes. How can he not know that cantaloupes are to be sniffed, not squeezed. Men! With your quintessential blunt cut college 'do' swinging, Lauren sweats and Reeboks, you stride over confidently, pausing briefly to gaze at the surface of the meat scale to check your make up.

"I dumped my last boyfriend for that", you toss in nonchalantly, at once piqueing his curiosity, demonstrating your current availability, your knowledge of cantaloupe testing and your assertiveness.

"Always sniff a cantaloupe."

Toss a couple of ripe ones into his basket and give him one of those looks like fishing weights are tugging at your eyelids. The heavier the weights, the more likely he is to follow up. Keep a stack of cards handy with your number.

The Squash Ladder

What better way to flash those cellulite-free thighs at the stud of your dreams than to take to the squash court. Sign up on the ladder using a variant of your name that could pass for a man's. Try Billy for Billie, Jack for Jackie or Sam for Samantha. Show up a bit late and head to the viewing area so you can check out the goods on this week's opponent/potential date. If he is a total gweeb, head back to the ladder and switch the match so that he thinks he had the wrong time.

If he fits the bill, smooth your shorts and head down to the court. Maintain just the right mix of competence and helplessness, working your way through to the end of the game. Caution: if you play a strong game, beware the fragile male ego. Or what the hell, whip his ass! Whatever the score, be sure to bet dinner and a movie on it. You can't lose.

The Chemistry Lab

Best locale to select a future doctor with strong anatomy skills. Be sure to wear enough perfume to overpower the paradichlorobenzene. Spend the extra few bucks to get yourself a set of lab glasses that don't leave you looking like something from a Herman cartoon. Although you will have to wear a lab coat, whose to be the wiser if you take up the hem a few inches? Position yourself across from the chemist of your choice and set up your flasks and glassware with a studied coolness.

As you begin your titration, gaze through your graduated cylinder and try to meet his glance between the 50 cc and 75 cc gradations. Try a topical approach, something like "Pass the Carbon Tetrachloride, please". Continue to distil and decant for a while before lowering your glasses slightly and asking him over to compare notes. No catalyst required.

The Bus Stop

There's nothing special about bus stops, but what the hell, wherever it is that he is heading, he may need a bus to get there. If you can borrow daddy's Mercedes coupe on a rainy day, you can go for the direct approach. Pull up at the stop, roll down the passenger side window and ask whether the fine specimen is heading up to campus. Be sure to liberally salt in some comments about how you can't believe that you are doing this, so that he doesn't get the idea that you do this often or that you read it in a book or something.

Daddy is out of town, high local crime rate or no Mercedes? Try hanging out at the stop yourself. Ask for some directions. Work the directions into some light conversation about the pace of buses. As the bus finally pulls up, drop whatever you can onto the ground. As he bends down to pick up your gear, check to see whether baldness runs in his family. Little thin up there? He must be using his hormones for something else. Head for a double seat and share your chocolate bar.

Part Three – Where to Take 'em

While most aspects of dating have changed dramatically over the years, the bad news is that the battle still rages over who should pay. On a student budget that can be a painful experience. However, by playing the odds you can avoid looking cheap and save yourself a heap of cash in the interim. The trick is, always be the first to offer to pay. After you offer, pray that an "Oh no, I insist" will come back. Shrug sheepishly and find something to do with your hands as your date whips out the Gold Amex.

Naturally you will need some 'show money' to bluff your way through. Borrow a handful of twenties from a rich friend and flash them around as you offer to pay. No bite? Simply say thanks. You're stuck. But it's worth a try.

Whoever pays, you will need to have a few ideas for cheap dates that will enhance your image of spartan sophistication. Here are five destinations that will advance you to unparalleled popularity.

The Zoo

Ideal as an initial exploratory outing. By closely monitoring your date, you will get an initial pulse on the relationship. Which animals does your date show the most interest in? Any similarities? Hmmm. Note any reaction to those animals with baby animals in the family. In tune with your own? Does your date have pig-like qualities (eating the stale bread and popcorn rather than feeding it to the zoo residents)? What was the reaction when he baboons began mating? Appalled and disgusted? Intrigued and drew you closer? Salivated and pawed at you frantically? Check your social calendar for next week.

The Drive-In Movie

Ah yes, the drive-in movie. The romance magnet from our parent's era, where guys and girls went to enjoy a movie, split a Cherry Coke, wolf down bags of buttery popcorn and do some serious frenching and groping. Today, under a thin veil of nostalgia and on a student budget, you can enjoy a movie, split a Diet Pepsi, nibble on some no-salt-no-butter popcorn and do some serious frenching and groping. And yes, scary films are still the best. Don't forget the blanket.

The Art Gallery

Best for, you guessed it, the artsie types. As with any other activity, best to do a little prep work so that you view the works right side up and don't leave your cigarette butts in the statues. Practice the terminology a bit as well. 'Works', not 'paintings'. 'It's a look', rather than 'it sucks'.

"Perhaps one of her earlier pieces", as opposed to, "Was this done by an eight year old?"

Stare at each piece sagely for about twice as long as it takes to get more than bored with it. A slight nodding of the head will make your date aware that you *know* art and build the necessary authenticity to make the old line about coming up to see your etchings work.

The Picnic

The venerable old ham and mayo sandwich is transformed into the basis of a romantic renaissance by a checkered table cloth, a big bottle of cheap wine and a dollop of pate. Somewhere between the black fly bites and the incessant buzzing of the crickets the relationship is bound to grow, like the soft fuzzy green moss on the cheese that you forgot to inspect ahead of time. Load up on the cheap but impressive stuff: an old candle or two, a couple of kiwis, a bunch of grapes and a baguette. By slicing some ham into long strips and sprinkling it with Tabasco, you can probably pawn it off as Prosciutto. With your trusty old *Best of Bread* tape crooning softly on your ghetto blaster, something akin to love is bound to develop.

The Athletic Event

Pick an activity where you have some level of skill. Borrow the necessary rock climbing, windsurfing, parachuting, hang gliding or spelunking equipment and head for the best cliff, waves, airport, mountain or cave in the area and have at it. An old bandanna will help to mop the sweat and some sun screen will help to keep the ozone from breaking down your date's bodily defences before you do. A six pack of Bud chilling on ice in your trunk will keep the moment fresh and special after you have climbed, sailed, fallen, soared and explored your little hearts out.

Summary

Almost anyone can find a date with a little work and an original approach. Most people have had it with cliche pick up lines and lukewarm follow through. Work in a little sizzle with the steak and enjoy the best dating years of your life. Suburbia is just around the corner...!

2 BEYOND THE CARE PACKAGE

– a guide to eating cheap

Eight PM. Exhausted, frustrated, smelly and starving. It has been a helluva day. You handed in your Chemistry lab late and you got back your Math midterm. The professor had marked it in binary rather than in decimal numbers since, she claimed, that was the most efficient way of representing your sub-optimal grade. Your Anthropology assignment due tomorrow, exists only as pristine, white sheets of paper, and not yet relegated to the darkness of the plastic cover that you have so lovingly picked out for it. The truth is painful, but unavoidable: you haven't started it yet.

The weight of your ill-compiled BASIC program strains the stitching on your knapsack and carves two neat grooves in your shoulders as you continue your trudge home. Darkness begins to fall. The rhythm of your heels on the side walk provides a welcome numbing effect to the grizzly events of the day. Your mind searches to find something pleasurable to graze on, some kind of refreshing change from the misery that it has now accepted as reality.

Yesterday's visit from your parents springs to mind. Being with them was an escape back to simpler times. They acted surprisingly normal and didn't make too many comments about your hairstyle, the rips in your jeans, your opposite sex roommates or the apparent cyclone that had mysteriously swept through your apartment. The whole day was a relief from the pressures offered by the daily grind. It was clear they were proud of you for your successes at school so far, although you weren't certain that surprised wasn't the more accurate verb.

Naturally, the best part of the visit was the leftover steak and scalloped potatoes that your mom had brought. It seems that they had organized your birthday dinner last week without you being there. It was a little depressing, but at least they had been kind enough to reward you with the leftovers, including the desert: Mom's own apple pie.

Suddenly, things are looking up. You adjust the knapsack on your shoulders and your sneakers seem to bound effortlessly toward your apartment. It seems as though a tail wind had developed, helping you on your way. Since it is only a quarter past eight, you would still have time for dinner. Best of all, with mom's leftovers safely in the fridge, there would actually be something to eat. After dinner there would still be time to work on your Anthropology assignment, you kid yourself, knowing that M.A.S.H. will be on at 9:30. A growl from your stomach reminds you that lunch was a long time ago and there is still fifteen minutes of walking ahead.

Wait. What is that up ahead, just above the sidewalk? Steam was rising gently from a huge steak, smothered in mushroom sauce. Nestled next to it was a veritable mountain range of scalloped potatoes. The smells wafted temptingly toward you as your eyes strain at the vision ahead. Yes. It is a plate of apple pie heated up with a ball of ice cream crouched down, slowly surfing on the crust.

With a shake of your head, the image is gone. Picking up the pace, you jog the last few blocks home.

You hear the sound of the television from your apartment as you bound up the steps. The scene in the kitchen enrages you. The tiny bits of charred black steak on your roommate's face provide the overview. The scalloped potato stains on his shirt fill in the details. His cheeks, stuffed to the limit with apple pie and ice cream, form the conclusive evidence.

A Guide to Eating Cheap

Roommates can never be trusted fully, and high-grade leftovers can stress even the closest of friendships, as year end budgets run dry and all roommates stake the claim on that last box of Kraft Dinner that silently stands guard over the barren, paint chipped surfaces that make up your cupboards. Food can take a low priority when assignments and exams compete for your attention and even washroom breaks need to be booked two weeks in advance.

To keep 'borrowing' roommates at bay, try booby trapping one or two fridge items to teach 'em a lesson. Punch a hole in the bottom of a beer can and fill it up with pickle juice, covering the hole with some duct tape. Inject that last piece of chocolate cake with dish soap. Be sure to keep a mental map of what is still safe.

Balancing that delicate line between the truly cheap and tasteless and the pricey yet palatable can prove to be a tenuous task. Once again, luckily, you have come to the right book to find all the answers.

This chapter is divided into three sections to suit both your tastes and your pocket book. If you find yourself constantly in a hurry, and the queens, kings or presidents on the bills squint when you open your wallet, you will want to prepare most of your chow from the Survival Rations section. The stuff requires minimal ingredients and can be prepared and wolfed down in less than ten minutes in most cases. These delightful dishes will likely keep you going all term provided you stock up on some vitamin pills, avoid excessive exertion and get plenty of rest. If signs of scurvy or rickets appear, or if anything swells up or becomes discoloured, see your doctor, shell out the extra cash for ingredients and move up to the next level and prepare to enjoy the Palate Pleasers.

The Palate Pleasers are a collection of college favourites that require a little planning, a working stove and a touch of your personal artistry. They will also require a few ingredients that can bump the cost per serving up beyond one dollar. Some of these creations even taste good. The food will keep you happy and healthy and even mom would approve of the nutrient value.

For those occasions where you need to prepare the very best, flip ahead to the Haute Cuisine section. There you will find the simmering sauces, the ominous omlettes and the flaming fantasies that you will need to ensure the dedication from that dreamboat that you met through the methods that I outlined in Chapter 1.

For generations, people have been on the quest for the food that is the perfect aphrodisiac. Key point to remember: If the student you are chasing is as broke and as starving as you, *any* food will be an aphrodisiac. If nothing else, it will encourage them to keep coming over, if only to eat.

Simple as that. Check your budget, know your tastes and turn the section that suits your habits the best. And, oh yes, Bon Appétit!

The Basics

Before we don our aprons and start spraying flour around the kitchen, lets lay out some basic ground rules and concepts to make the work as simple as possible. These tips will apply to all three levels of cuisine.

Measurement

Cooking can often involve the combination of two or more ingredients to create the new substance that you will learn to eat. More often than not, it is useful to use the appropriate amount of reagents to create your dish. Most cookbooks will tell you what to put in, but they will use ridiculous units of measure like tbsp's, tsp's, cups and the like. The whole thing is a scam.

Throughout this chapter, we will use three units of measure. One is the coffee mug, which I will refer to as 'a mug'. Second unit is 'the spoon'. What kind of spoon? It doesn't matter. Just a spoon. The third type of measure is 'some'. As in "Add some salt". Or, "Add some vinegar". A couple of good shakes of whatever is dispensing the ingredient ought to do it. Most people cook far too precisely anyway. Quick review – a mug, a spoon and some. Great!

Tools

There are a few items that you will need to create your new gourmet masterpieces, particularly those that will require some cooking. I will keep the list to a minimum, but if you can load up with all of the items below, you will be able to make everything in this chapter. For most of these items, scour the basement, mom probably has duplicates gathering dust. If you strike out in the basement, you can probably buy everything that you will need at a garage sale, flea market or at one of those discount stores.

1. BIG POT. Get one ten or more inches in diameter and five or more inches high. A matching lid will be especially handy. Stainless steel (shiny silver look) is the best since it cleans easily, distributes heat well and is easy to clean. Aluminum ones (not as shiny) will do the job, but they can be tougher to clean. Make sure that your roomates don't rinse out their swim suits in this baby.

2. REGULAR POT. About eight or nine inches around and four inches deep with a handle out one side and a matching lid. Again, stainless steel is the best, aluminum will do.

3. PYREX PAN. These are square or rectangular clear glass pans that say Pyrex on the bottom. The nine by thirteen inch size is the best, but you can probably live with a nine by nine inch one.

4. FRYING PAN. Get one ten to twelve inches in diameter, ideally one of the Teflon coated or Silverstone ones. They are easy to clean. Just don't scratch the surface by using metal implements with it.

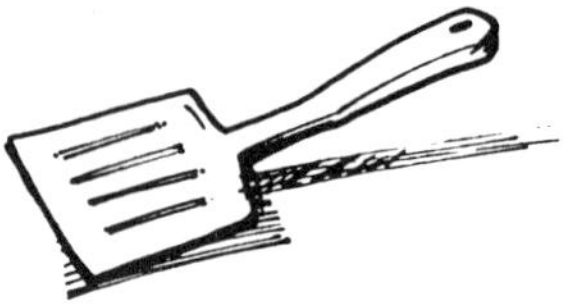

5. FLIPPER (a.k.a. a spatula). Plastic ones are the best since you won't scratch your nice teflon pans.

6. WOODEN SPOON. Yup, just like the one that grandma used to use on your backside. Check the basement again or pick one up cheap at the corner store.

7. STRAINER. Get a plastic one at a grocery or kitchen store. These babies are indispensable for draining noodles and things. (If you progress to the Haute Cuisine section, you will learn to call it pasta, but for now, we can run with noodles.) In a pinch, you can use an old tennis or squash racket.

8. PLASTIC LEFTOVER CONTAINERS. These aren't essential, but they are handy for saving your leftovers and keeping the green suede off them. Tupperware works well, as do any of the sets available at the grocery store. Or use an old yogurt container.

9. TIN FOIL. Get a big roll to keep you going all term. Very useful when roasting things in your new Pyrex pan.

10. A TOASTER. What better way to make toast? If you can't get one for free, try rummaging around at some garage sales until you find one that you like. Be sure to plug it in to make sure that it heats up, before you buy.

11. A SHARP KNIFE. One with a smooth sharp blade about eight inches long will do the trick.

12. A SERVING CLOTH. A white towel from the Recreation Centre that needs to be replaced every month, or when it turns grey, whichever comes first.

Cleanup Tips

Following are a few ideas to help you forge your way through the mountains of grimy dishes that can result from all of this cooking:

1. While waiting for something to finish cooking, take a moment to clean up your work area, wash any utensils and at least get the major items soaking.

2. Never leave an item to dry out, harden and endure a metamorphosis to something unworldly, especially things like sauces and noodle pots. They can become virtually impossible to clean. Get everything soaking as soon as possible after completion of the meal.

3. For really tough pots, scrape the major hunks out with a spoon and let the pot soak for at least one hour with hot water and dish soap. Then try to clean it with one of those plastic bristle scrubbers. If that doesn't do it, try putting a little dish soap and a couple mugs of water in it and let it cook on a low element for an hour. Or try a few spoonfuls of baking soda and a couple of mugs of water. Bring to a boil and watch the brown scrunge bubble up. Don't forget about it! Then try the scrubber again. Should do it.

4. Keep things moist while you are cooking them. If something starts to look dry or smell burnt, add some water to unstick it from the pan and re-moisten the food.

That's it. You are ready to begin.

Survival

You only foray into a kitchen to grab a beer? You think that the Cloves of Garlic are some sort of a religious order? Compote was the guy who wrote the murder mysteries? OK. No need for panic, you have come to the right place. This is the section designed for the gastronomically inept and the constantly broke.

The Fried Egg Sandwich

I can almost taste it now. I know that it doesn't sound like much, but give it a try. They are tasty and the total ingredient cost for this breakfast/lunch/dinner is about thirty cents.

Ingredients:

One Egg
Some Mayonnaise (if you are asking how much is 'some' you need to re-read the beginning of this chapter).
Two slices of Brown Bread (the white stuff is for wimps).
Some Pepper and Salt.
Some Butter.

Tools:

Fry pan.
Flipper.
Stove that works.

Directions:

Timing is everything. Turn on your stove to medium high (or about six on a scale from one to nine. Place your frying pan on the heated element and add some butter about the size of a quarter. Wait for it to start swimming around. As soon as it moves, drop your bread in the toaster and turn it on. Run back to the stove and you should see the butter starting to bubble. As soon as it does, crack the egg into the pan and use the corner of your flipper to break the yolk so that the yellow part runs into the white part. Shake some salt and pepper on the gooey part. Give it a minute or so and then slide under the egg with your flipper and flip it. Turn off the element, run over to the toaster, remove the bread and slather some mayonnaise on one piece. Scoop up your egg with your flipper and lay it on the bread and then quickly cover it with the other piece of bread. Wolf it down quickly while it is still hot. Awesome.

Kraft Dinner

What chapter on student cuisine could be complete without directions for making Kraft Dinner? I will even include some tips for improving it that even the people from Kraft won't tell you.

Ingredients:

One box of Kraft Dinner
Some Hot Dogs (optional, but a big improvement over plain KD)
Some Butter
Some Powdered Onion Soup Mix (optional, but again a real enhancement)
Some Milk.

Tools:

A regular pot
A plastic strainer
A wooden spoon

Directions:

Turn one of your stove elements to high (or nine or ten or Max). Pour four mugs of water into your regular pot and place it on the heated element. Take some hot dogs and slice them into pieces about one inch long and set them off to one side. Add some salt to the water in the pot. When the water boils (big bubbles in the water and lots of steam rising), open the box of Kraft Dinner and remove the cheese sauce mix. Dump noodles and sliced hot dogs into the boiling water and let the whole works boil for about twelve minutes or until the noodles are tender.

If you are not sure when they are done, just pull one out with your wooden spoon, blow on it to cool, and then taste it. Optionally, you can toss a noodle against a wall. If it sticks it's done. If it falls off the wall, try giving it another couple of minutes. By using the toss method on a regular basis, you will have a post modern pasta sculpture on the wall by the time you graduate. When the noodles are ready, turn the element to low, remove the pot from the heat and dump noodles and dogs into the strainer which should be sitting in the sink. Run some hot water over the noodles and dogs while they are in the strainer to wash off all of the, well, whatever it is that needs to be washed off.

Now, add some butter to the bottom of the empty, but still hot, pot and place it back on the element that you have turned down to low heat. Dump the rinsed and drained noodles and dogs back into the pot. Open the cheese sauce mix package and dump it in too. Add ⅛ of a mug of milk and stir the whole works up until there are no big bright orange globs of cheese sauce mix. Now here's the trick. Toss in about ⅛ of a mug of Powdered Onion Soup Mix and stir it in as well. Serves two. Lovely.

Leftovers? No problem. Dump the extras into your handy plastic containers and stick the whole works right into the fridge.

Salade Estudentee

How about a little side salad to go with your main dish? Also, not a bad idea to at least have a few vegetables hanging around, just in case your parents come to visit. Whatever your motives, you are looking for an easy to make salad with dressing. You have truly arrived when you can master the Salade Estudentee.

Ingredients:

Some Lettuce
A Green Pepper
A Tomato
Some Celery
Some of whatever other Vegetables you can find.
Some Ketchup
Some Olive Oil (the oil and vinegar are expensive, but they will probably last you all year).
Some Salt
Some Sugar
Some Wine Vinegar (plain white vinegar is for washing windows)

Tools:

A plastic strainer
A sharp knife
A coffee mug

Directions:

Give all of your vegetables a good washing with cold water to remove all of the crud that may have become lodged on them during transit. Rip off small pieces of the lettuce and toss it into your plastic strainer in the sink. Slice the green pepper in half and pull out all of the seedy parts in the middle and pitch them in the garbage. Rinse out the insides and then slice the pepper into lengthwise strips and then cross wise to make little squares about one half inch. Put the pepper squares into the plastic strainer with the lettuce.

Pull the green thing out of the end of your tomato and slice it in half from where you pulled out the green thing to the other 'pole' of the tomato. Place the two halves face down and slice 'em in half again. Repeat one more time. Now turn these wedges sideways and cut them each into four pieces. Throw the works into your plastic strainer.

Slice the last inch off each end of your celery and throw them out. Slice the remaining stalk into thin slices crosswise and toss them in the strainer. As a rule of thumb, the harder the vegetable (carrots or celery) the smaller the slices so that you don't ruin your dental work or that of your dinner guests.

For the dressing, you can save money by making your own. In a coffee mug, pour one quarter mug of ketchup, one quarter mug of water, one spoon of sugar, one spoon of wine vinegar, one spoon of olive oil and some salt. Stir the whole works up and presto, you have dressing.

Toss the vegetables around in the strainer with your hands, put some in a bowl and splash some of your dressing on top. Excellent. For variety, try throwing some grated cheese and sliced ham on top. Don't forget to keep the leftovers in your plastic food savers in the fridge.

Le Fishstick

Ahh, the salt spray, the Rhyme of the Ancient Mariner or perhaps an old Gilligan's Island episode have got you in the mood for some fruits of the sea. Never mind the idea that you can't afford seafood. Le Fishstick is an easy, economical way to enjoy the catch of the day.

Ingredients:

One box of Frozen Fish Sticks

Tools:

Some tinfoil
An oven

Directions:

Heat the oven up to 350°F. From your box of frozen fish sticks, remove as many as you think you can eat. Set them on a sheet of tin foil, shiny side up. Wrap the foil over top of the fish sticks to make a neat little package with the shiny side of the foil facing inward to the fish sticks. Put the whole works on the rack in the oven for twenty minutes. Remove and taste a little piece. If they are still cold, send them back in for another fifteen minutes. If they are warm, but not hot, try ten minutes. If in doubt, read the directions on the box.

When they are fully heated, serve them up on a plate. You might want to make a little seafood sauce by combining ⅛ of a mug of relish with ⅛ of a mug of mayonnaise. Try serving with Salade Estudentee as a side dish.

Palate Pleasers

Got a little more time on your hands. A little extra cash. Eaten all the recipes in the Survival Rations section twelve times? Lost more than ten pounds? Sounds like you're ready for the Palate Pleasers – a selection of recipes as delightful to make as they are to eat. Here we go.

Spuds Nicoise

Potatoes are incredibly cheap, nourishing and filling. In short, its a good idea to keep a big bag of 'em handy. The possibilities are endless, so I will give you the basics and a few variations to get you started...

Ingredients:

Some Spuds (I prefer the red skins)
Some Butter
Some Cheese OR

Some Barbecue Sauce OR
Ketchup and Soy Sauce mix (60:40) OR
Some Sour Cream or Yogurt

Tools:

Big pot
Plastic strainer
Frying pan

Directions:

Fill the big pot one third full of water and set it on a burner at high heat. Add a sprinkle of salt to the water. While waiting for the water to boil, wash the spuds under cool water and use a plastic dish scrubber to clean off all the dirt. If they are really filthy, you may have to change the water and give them a second scrubbing. Cut the potatoes once lengthwise and once width wise, leaving them, you guessed it, in quarters. When the water is boiling, add potato quarters until the water comes within about 2" of the top edge of the pot. Leave the spuds to boil for about 20 minutes or until a fork slides in fairly easily. Don't let them get mooshy.

When they are cooked, turn the burner down to medium high and dump the spuds out into your plastic strainer in the sink and let them dry out a bit. Toss a spoonful of butter into your frying pan and set it on that medium high burner. Slice the quartered potatoes into thinner wedges, letting them fall into the frying pan. Turn them every couple of minutes or so, adding extra butter to the pan if they start to burn. Or turn down the heat. Sprinkle on some salt and pepper. When they are all nice and golden brown you have a number of options:

Option 1.

Lay some slices of cheese on them and let the cheese melt. Serve.

Option 2.

Douse them in barbecue sauce. Serve.

Option 3.

Douse them in sour cream or plain yogurt. Serve.

The possibilities are endless. Almost anything that you can find in your fridge can be drizzled on top. Create your own spud sensations.

KD Casserole for Two

Aha! You recognize the initials KD as standing for Kraft Dinner and you are indeed very observant. This little charmer is likely to really blow your guests away. Not much tougher to make than regular KD either.

Ingredients

2 mugs of Frozen Mixed Vegetables (the California ones with the cauliflower, crinkle cut carrots and broccoli are the best, but any kind, including the good ole peas, carrots and corn, will do)
1 box of Kraft Dinner
Some Crackers (regular Saltines, graham, Bretons, whatever)
Some Cheese (whatever you got – parmesan, cheddar, swiss, whatever)
Some Butter

Tools:

Big pot
Pyrex pan
Plastic Strainer
Oven

Directions:

Fill your big pot about ½ full of water. Add a dash of salt and turn the oven burner to its maximum heat. While waiting for the water to boil, open the box of Kraft Dinner and remove the envelope with the cheese sauce mix. Set it aside. Measure out 2 mugs of frozen mixed vegetables and set them aside (either in two coffee mugs or in a bowl.)

When the water reaches a boil, dump in the box of Kraft Dinner noodles, and note the time. Give it a stir every now and again to keep the little suckers from sticking to the bottom of the pot (they will anyway). After six minutes, dump in the two mugs of frozen vegetables, and give everything another six minutes to boil and swap flavours. Turn off the burner you were using and set the oven to 350°F.

Dump the cooked vegetables and the noodles into your plastic strainer and give them a good rinse with hot water. Add a spoonful of butter to your big pot and dump the noodles and the vegetables back in along with the contents of the cheese sauce mix packet. Add ¼ mug of milk and mix it in as well. Yum. Give it a good stir. Take out your Pyrex pan and dump the contents of your big pot into it, spreading it all around so that it is an even depth throughout. Crumble your crackers in your hand and sprinkle them on top of the noodles and vegetables in the pan. If the cheese you are using is already in small particles (like powdered Parmigiana) sprinkle it evenly on top of the crackers, otherwise, slice the cheese into fine strips and lay the strips evenly on top of the crackers. Put the pan in the oven and leave it for fifteen minutes, or until the cheese is melted on top.

Turn the oven off and use a towel to remove your casserole from the oven. Serve it onto plates using your flipper, making sure that you get enough cracker and cheese topping for both you and your guest. Enjoy!

Bluefish Fettucini

OK, I lied. Le Fishstick are starting to taste like nothing more than frozen fish sticks and you are hungering for some REAL seafood. Naturally, your budget is no better and your cooking skills are still less than world class. Bluefish Fettucini will fool them every time. It is a similar concept to KD Casserole and just as easy. The beauty of it is that it uses skills that you have already developed (boiling and stirring) and yet it will let you to dramatically expand your repertoire. Let's begin...

Ingredients

1 Package of Frozen Bluefish Fillets (I use Highliner brand) be sure to defrost them in the fridge overnight
4 mugs of Noodles (any kind will do, check the Italian section of your grocery store and buy a big bag).
1 mug of Milk
Some Butter
Some Salt
1 small can of Mushroom Soup

Tools:

Big pot
Medium pot
Plastic strainer

Directions:

Turn one of your stove burners on to its maximum setting. Oh yeah. You are probably wondering how much this recipe will make. I don't know. I could swear I use the same amount of ingredients every time and sometimes there is enough for just me and sometimes I fill up a couple of those plastic storage containers. If you are feeding two or three, you should be OK. If you are feeding four, maybe toss in an extra mug of noodles.

Fill your big pot approximately ½ full of water and set it on the element to boil. While you are waiting for the water to boil, measure out 4 mugs of noodles and set them aside. Turn a second burner to its low setting and add one mug of milk, the can of mushroom soup and the bluefish fillets. Stir gently so that the fish, the milk and the mushroom soup meld together into an ambrosial delight. Add salt and pepper to taste. If this sauce starts to bubble heavily, turn it down a notch or two. Don't forget to give it a stir every now and again, or it will become a charred meltdown.

The water in the big pot is probably boiling furiously by now. Great. Dump in your four mugs of noodles boiling them for about 20 minutes or until they taste about right (not too hard, not too mooshy).

When the noodles are done, turn off the burner you were using to boil them on and turn the sauce burner up to about mid way. Dump your noodles into your plastic strainer and give them a good rinse with hot water. Shake them vigorously to remove all the excess water. Load the noodles onto plates and add a good sized dollop of your Blue fish sauce on top. Serve with a cold glass of beer. Superb.

Gotta Lasagna

Perfezione! Time for a little Italiano cuisine. Here is a lasagna that isn't terribly quick to make, but it is nutritious, tasty and it will keep you fed for at least a week. Or if you entertaining dinner guests, this will do for about six of 'em. If you are considering this for a special date with your newest heart throb, trust me. Nothing is a surer route to someone's heart than a good home made lasagna.

Ingredients

1 bag of Lasagna Noodles (the broad flat ribbon ones)
1 small can of Mushroom Soup (good to toss in to almost anything)
1 big jar of Spaghetti Sauce (ideally, get one with mushrooms and all the trimmings)
1 good sized package of Mozzarella Cheese (take your calculator and work out the unit cost on this stuff – it's always a rip off)
1 spoon of Butter

Tools:

Big pot
Medium pot
Plastic strainer
Wooden spoon

Directions:

Fill your big pot ½ full of water, on a stove burner set to high. Drop one spoonful of butter into the water. This will help to keep the noodles from sticking together. While waiting for it to boil, dump your mushroom soup and spaghetti sauce into your medium pot and add about ½ mug of water. Set it on another burner at medium-low heat. Keep stirring it until the mushroom soup, water and the spaghetti sauce all blend together nicely.

As soon as the water starts boiling in the big pot, put the lasagna noodles in. Don't tell me, let me guess. Your noodles won't fit in the pot. I've been there, don't panic. Put them in with one end sticking out and give them about a minute to soften up. Push on the exposed end and you should find that they will coil around inside the pot until they are all submerged. Be careful not to burn your fingers while you are noodle wrestling. Give the noodles a stir with your wooden spoon.

Now while everything is boiling and simmering nicely, turn your oven on to 350°F. Take out your Pyrex pan and smear butter all over the inside of it with your fingers. Wash your hands well. Slice your Mozzarella cheese into thin slices and set aside. Don't forget to keep stirring your sauce to make sure it isn't sticking to the bottom. But it will.

When the noodles have been boiling for about 15 minutes, start tasting them to check for consistency. Toss one against the wall to work on your sculpture. You want them cooked all the way through and just a bit chewy in the centre. When they are done, dump them into your plastic strainer in the sink and rinse them well with warm water.

Now comes the fun part. Lay one layer of noodles in the bottom of your Pyrex pan. If they don't fit, rip off the excess. You can use it somewhere else later. Scoop a nice layer of sauce on top of the noodles. Now, run the next layer of noodles the other direction to help give your lasagna some structural integrity (like plywood). Continue alternating layers of sauce and noodles until:

1. You run out of sauce.
2. You run out of noodles.
3. You get bored.
4. You are dying to find out how the sliced cheese works into all of this.
5. The pan is almost full.

Here comes the cheese. Over your last layer, add a layer of sliced Mozzarella cheese. Alright, you say, should I be adding the cheese on top of a layer of noodles or on top of a layer of sauce. There are actually two schools of thought on this, but I would recommend adding the cheese onto the sauce layer. Don't sweat it if you ran out of sauce and had to run the cheese on top of the noodles.

With all of your layers done, open the oven and slide in your lasagna onto a rack on about the middle level. Leave it in there for about 15 minutes or before smoke billows out of the oven. Remove using a heavy towel. Cut into squares with a knife and use your flipper to serve it onto plates. Serve with cold beer.

Haute de Cuisine

Ha! You laugh. Those recipes are hardly food. There must be life beyond noodles. Perhaps your budget is somewhat more liberal with your paltry student loan being sautéed with a hefty trust fund from Uncle Reginald. Perhaps your tastes yearn for the kinds of cuisine that you recall from your parent's country club. You recall how the grapefruit sorbet crisply cleansed your palate from the

Cornish hens and the wild rice, how Bif brushed Daddy's best polo pony, how the afternoon sun glinted between the tiers of the split rail fence...

Alas, those days are gone and you are left to fend for yourself in the condo that your parents have bought you near the school. With no servants you are actually left to cook for yourself. The following will describe breakfast, dinner and desert that will get you through the term.

Ominous Omelette

Having selected a leisurely program since you have a guaranteed spot in the family enterprise anyway, you have the time to lounge and enjoy a decent breakfast. How about a superb omelette to savour as you peruse the stock market tables in the morning paper?

Ingredients:

2 Eggs
Some Spaghetti Sauce
Some whole fresh Mushrooms, Green Peppers and Onions
Some Cheese (whatever kind you may have handy)
1 spoonful of Butter

Tools:

Fry pan
Medium pot
FlipperBowl

Directions:

In your medium pot, pour about ½ a mug of spaghetti sauce and set to warm on a medium-low burner. Slice up about 3 mushrooms, some slivers of green pepper and onion into thin slices and drop them into the sauce. Give the whole works a stir.

Put a small spoonful of butter into your frying pan and set it on a medium-high burner. Crack two eggs into a bowl and beat them feverishly with a fork. When the butter melts and starts to bubble, pour in your freshly beaten eggs. Give the omelette about 2 minutes to cook and then use your flipper to gently work the edges of the omelette free. After about 3 minutes, slide your flipper under the whole omelette and carefully flip it over.

Pour your sauce over one side of the omelette near one side of the pan and use your flipper to roll the sauce-loaded part over itself. Continue rolling it until the whole omelette is like a tube with the sauce inside. Roll it right out of the pan and on to your plate. Serve with a sprig of parsley and a Perrier.

Lemon, Lime and Lager Chicken

The ruins of our capitalist society. I can't believe that I am selling out. Making my Lemon, Lime and Lager Chicken recipe available to the masses. Such are the things that one has to do to cope with our tax system and the realities of a mortgage...

... A splendid chicken dish that will leave you (or your guests) duelling for more. You might want to consider cooking up some rice as a side dish and really dazzling your guests with the desert that follows. Serves four. Bon Appétit à quatre.

Ingredients:

4 skinless Chicken Breasts
Some Lemon Juice
Some Marmalade
1 Lemon
1 Lime
Some Lemon Juice
Some Lime Juice (in one of those fake plastic limes)
Some Beer (white wine will work too or whatever you have left over from your last soirée)
Some Corn Starch (this stuff will thicken anything)
Some Sour Cream or Plain Yogurt

Tools:

Pyrex pan
Tin Foil
Flipper
Sharp knife

Directions:

Set the oven to 350°F. Remove any excess fat from the chicken using a sharp knife. Lay the chicken breasts into the Pyrex pan bony side down. Pour about ¼ mug of lemon juice, ¼ mug of lime juice and 1 mug of beer or white wine into the pan over the chicken. Blob in 4 heaping spoonfuls of marmalade. Sprinkle in some salt and pepper.

Use a sheet of tin foil to cover the chicken (shiny side toward the chicken). Tuck the foil in around the edges to ensure a good seal. Put the pan in the oven on a rack somewhere near the middle.

Meanwhile, slice up the lemons and limes into wheels about ¼" thick. Set them aside. When the chicken has cooked for about ½ hour, carefully remove the tin foil and use a knife to make a small incision in the chicken. If the juice is clear it is done. If the juice is pink and the veins are still visible, give it another five minutes or so.

Use a spoon to spread some marmalade over the chicken, remove the foil and set the oven control to broil. Slide the pan back in and let it broil for about 4 minutes with the rack set so that the tops of the chicken is about 6" from the element. Pull it out again, lay the lemon and lime slices over the chicken and add a little more marmalade onto the slices. Slide the works back into the oven for about another 2 minutes.

Pour off the remaining juices from the pan into a glass and skim off any fat. In a mug, mix one heaping spoonful of corn starch with enough cold water to make a paste. Add some sour cream or yogurt to make it totally awesome. Combine the cornstarch paste and the remaining chicken cooking juices in a frying pan on low heat, stirring constantly until it begins to thicken. Don't boil it or it will get lumpy.

Remove the chicken from the Pyrex pan and position nicely on plates with the lemon and lime garnishes. Pour some of the sauce over the chicken. Add a side dish of rice or noodles. Serve with a glass of Dom Perignon.

Flaming Cointreau Ice Cream

With such a scintillating entrée, only an equally dramatic desert would be fitting. Few can match the simplicity, elegance and gourmet flair of this delightful offering.

Ingredients:

Some Cointreau or virtually any liqueur that you have around

Some French Vanilla Ice Cream or virtually any kind you have lying around

Tools:

Frying pan
Matches
Fire Extinguisher

Directions:

Scoop some ice cream into each serving dish. Wet your spoon between scoops. Pour about ½ mug of Cointreau into the frying pan and heat over a low burner until you are overcome with fumes. Distribute the ice cream in dishes to your guests. After dimming the lights, light a match over the heated Cointreau and pour the flaming booze over the ice cream. Enjoy at once. Asbestos gloves optional, fire insurance recommended.

Got a student delicacy that I haven't covered? Send it along to the publisher, we'll get it in next time.

3 YOUR STUDENT HOVEL

– a primer on cockroaches, mice and leaks

Beer in hand, you saunter over to the couch to take a study break and watch some Flintstones reruns. The wool socks that Grandma gave you for Christmas seem to keep your feet reasonably warm despite widening holes induced by floor splinters and the Arctic freshness of your apartment.

HOLY $*%$&!@$%$%! A broken spring on the couch just pierced your jeans, sending you streaking to your feet. A warm trickle of blood tracks its way down your thigh. With the subsiding pain, you ponder the date of your last Tetanus shot. Ah well, with your schedule this term, there is no time for Tetanus shots anyway.

Settling back into the show and a safer spot on the couch, you are watching as Fred fastens Wilma's rock necklace before going to the Royal Order of the Water Buffalo Gala ball, when a mouse scoots in behind the... A mouse? A moouuusse? A MOUSE!!!

Racing to the broom closet in search of artillery, another floor splinter claims yet another victory in your sock. Where's the broom? Not surprisingly, it is occupying a lonely spot behind the more regularly used items – like skis, footballs, evil smelling gym bags, a twenty pound bag of mouldy spuds.

THE BROOM, THE BROOM.

The final tug that sets the broom free unleashes an avalanche of additional sporting goods from the straining shelf that held it all. Oh boy. This is going to take forever to... Later.

Incredibly, our rodent hero is still shadowboxing the dust bunnies lurking under the book shelf. A deft swat with the broom sends him scurrying along the baseboard, like an undersized, red-eyed greyhound in hot pursuit of an imaginary mechanical rabbit. You join the chase, stumbling over a stack of newspapers on the way to the kitchen. Where'd he go? Scanning the dust, the hair, and the dollops of spaghetti sauce that must have been left by the previous tenants, you suddenly resume eye contact.

The mouse dashes under the radiator. You wind up with your broom. You see the tail by the leg of the radiator. You feel your sinews straining your skin. You see his nose and whiskers brush by the radiator valve. Training your eye on the target and begining to unwind, you see the tiny claws attempt a final chin up on the pipe by the valve. As your torso twists, he turns to look, almost as if in dare. A swoosh of the broom, milliseconds to contact. The broom connects, sending both the radiator valve, the mouse and an unstoppable stream of water into orbit.

When the fire department arrives, explanations are difficult. Your mouth sputters only a stream of "I can't believe its" at the puddled floor.

The tenant in the apartment below was flooded out and assumed that sprinklers had gone off upstairs. Doing her civic duty, she had contacted the fire department to investigate. One by one the neighbours, the landlord, and then a bevy of curious onlookers gathered to savour the sight of a soul more desperate and wayward then their own. Few things brighten one's spirit like the regular reassurance that there others that are greater losers than oneself.

After carefully surveying the water, the pile of wet newspapers, the closet poltergeist and the throbbing crowds, one of the onlookers shook the water out of his fur, and silently scurried out the open door in search of cheese.

Finding a reasonable dwelling

While your student housing nightmares may not end up being quite this desperate, most students face some sort of housing problems during their years at school. Erratic heating and cooling systems, landlords who don't want to hear about mice, filth, fleas, noisy and/or slovenly and/or broke roommates, cockroaches, thieves, temperamental plumbing or electricity, rent increases or leaky roofs – can all add new dimensions to your school years.

Where to begin?

First decision is whether you can stay at home with the folks during your school years. Parents can be reasonable, but let's also be realistic. Are they going to understand when you come home covered in purple dye as a result of some orientation ritual? Will they be receptive to an impromptu Tequila shot party in their basement at 3 AM following a campus pub closing, with only fifty of your closest buddies in attendance? When you borrow your mom's best dress for the Halloween pub and it comes back marinated in beer, a buddy's vomit and the remnants of a chili dog, will she understand? Will she nod sagely and mutter things about how she remembers school too?

And what about you girls out there? Will you be able to bring home that long haired, rock singer that is soooooooo hunky to meet dad? Will dad demand his exit if your boyfriend asks where he can get a cardigan like your father's? Or will dad simply tell him where he got it and return to the development of his latest (and best) new trout fly?

Obviously, there are a number of critical questions that you must ask before entertaining the thought of living at home with your parents while going to school. Generally it boils down to simple arithmetic and geography. If you have money, you move out. If you don't and you live near school, you stay with your folks, save the cash and develop a sudden interest in making perogies and balloon curtains with mom and installing garage door openers and watching fishing shows with dad.

Shopping for an Apartment

As in all aspects of life, businesses will generally spring up poised to sap the cash from the uninformed, the desperate, the unfortunate, the about-to-become unfortunate and yes, even the student. I refer to those firms that specialize in locating accommodations for you, the starving student. There is absolutely no reason why you should pay someone to find you accommodations. There are a whole host of landlords out there looking for decent tenants such as yourself. All you have to do is find them and convince them of your decency.

Most colleges and universities have built-in accommodations called residences that provide some sort of shelter from the elements. More often than not they are equipped with running water. Some even have drains that work to carry all of this running water away. Kidding aside, residence accommodation may be the thing for you. It is cheap and often includes a deal on food-like substances that are dished out in a place called a cafeteria.

On the other hand, the rooms are the size of a Volkswagen trunk. The halls carry a continual stream of vocal excesses that can only come from those who are, apparently for the first time in their life, more than 10 feet from their parents' grasp. Never heed the student soothsayers and residence veterans who like to insist that the whole thing will quiet down into the term.

Residences also carry an institutional feel that is particularly disquieting. An institutional feel? Imagine living at a hospital and eating at the cafeteria, waiting to get your appendix out. Now imagine yourself staying there for three or four years. Let me add a couple more wrinkles. You are staying there while going to school, not waiting to have your appendix out. Get the idea? I, for one, cannot feel at home hearing my heels click on white tiles passing a janitor operating one of those huge floor polishers on the way to my sterile little room amidst a battalion of Neanderthal residence dwellers. That said, its up to you, they are cheap and liveable. For a year or two.

The university will, however, have a housing office where prospective landlords will post listings describing their offerings. I use the term 'describing' loosely since space is often at a premium and a listing will appear like:

> lvly thr bdrm twnhs ovrlkng lke wth w/o dck, stps t trnsprtn, bdrm whr ld, $335+, refs, frst, lst.

This one, for example, indicates a student ghetto type of row house that overlooks another row house where someone named

Mike apparently leaves his blinds open. There is some sort of deck out back that was probably added by city ordinance after a previous tenant twisted her ankle in a gopher hole. The hovel is within several thousand steps of public transportation and has no parking provisions. Broadloom is provided where laid, provided you provide and lay it. A panel of referees will scrutinize you and if you are the first one to show any interest, they will grab you. It is recommended that you do not speak with the tenant who was there last.

At any rate, make up a list of the features that you would like in and the features that you must have. (Laundry, public transportation, heat and hydro costs, parking etc.) Rank them in importance. On another piece of paper create a matrix with headings across the top for address, landlord's name, phone, rent and features. As you go through the listings posted at the housing office, jot down the addresses, landlord's names and numbers of the ones that look interesting. Find yourself a phone and call each, asking about the features and, if you are interested, when you can come to view the premises. If, for some reason, you couldn't get through, be sure to write down the reason – busy signal, landlord out, answering machine or someone else waiting for the pay phone who made you feel so guilty that you just couldn't make the last call or two.

The local newspapers are also a good source of housing opportunities with the one caveat that they may not be willing to rent to students. In most locales, this is contrary to human rights legislation, but try finding a lawyer who will fight it for free.

Back to the newspaper ads. The best time to tackle them is early on a Saturday morning and weeks before classes start. Most of the ads have just come out for the first time and you will have a chance to beat the thundering herds of students and apartment hunters that form your competition. You will get first crack at the pristine suites with a view of the beach below, the ocean breaking on the rocks, while you sip the bubbly in the salon, idly glancing at a text book. If nothing else, you will find a place with stains in the toilet bowl that can be scrubbed.

Steppin' Out

OK. I know the scene. You are a student right? You want to be comfortable, you want to look cool. Got the rips in the jeans, little mustard stain on the sweatshirt, no problems. I hear you. There's no need for the argyle socks and the bow tie, but you might want to spruce up your look just a little before you head out to meet your prospective new landlord. It's like anything else in life, sometimes you have to look the part that you aren't. And if a clean pair of jeans and a nice shirt is what it takes to land you the new pad that will make you the envy of your class, what the hell. Just wear some dark glasses so that no one recognizes you.

What To Look For

As you work your way through potential dwellings, look not only for the obvious, but for the subtle clues. Begin by taking a good whiff of the place. Damp? Mildew? Just because the place smells like the inside of a sail boat is no indication that you are headed for a spot on "Lifestyles of the Rich and Famous". It is virtually impossible to get rid of that odour which will eventually permeate everything that you own, including your stereo, your goldfish and your chemistry notes. There is also a reason why the smell is there to begin with. Check for water stains along the baseboards, on the ceilings or on the carpets, especially in basement locales. Any signs of dampness? Move on.

So the place seems reasonably dry and as you amble through checking out the details, you notice that the couple who came in after you seem to be quite keen. The place seems decent, what if they grab it before you do? Maybe you should... Hold it! Be honest. Was that you, mentally calculating the total of first and last month's rent. For shame. You haven't finished inspecting yet!

Open some cupboards in the kitchen. Any signs of mouse traps, roach motels or fly paper? Yech. It's enough of a jungle out there without having to fight the local wildlife for food from your own kitchen. Are the faucets leaking? If the faucets are leaking, how good is the landlord going to be about getting some heat going for you in February before you die of exposure? Is there adequate cupboard space in the off chance that a relative dies and bequeaths groceries to you?

Lets check out the bathroom. If there is going to be more than one of you living there, water pressure is going to be important. With two showers going, a load of laundry in and the kitchen tap leaking, someone is going to flush a toilet and leave your soap encrusted body to dry out in the shower for hours until someone else ends their water consuming activity.

To test the water pressure, try running the tap in the sink, start the shower and then flush the toilet. Still some water flowing in the shower? You are probably OK. Water go to a trickle or nothing at all? Could be problems. While you are in there, check for mildew. Mildew is the black, gooey stuff that tends to congregate in bathrooms between the tiles, or where the tiles meet the edge of the tub. In advanced stages, it can develop into moss or even lichens. At this point, it is your call. If it grew before, it might grow again. If it has advanced to the stage where you actually have small mushrooms sprouting from the grout, you should find yourself another place. What if your date saw such a bathroom? Besides, mother would be appalled.

With minimal vegetation in the bathroom, you can consider the bedroom. Is there ample room for your desk, bed and furniture? Can you hang more than two T shirts in the closet? Any signs of water damage on the ceiling that could indicate a leaky roof? Back to the closet for your now-routine check for mouse traps, roach motels and fly paper. Not to discriminate against other life forms. Some people don't seem to mind shared accommodation even when they thought they had the place to themselves. Still, nice to know what you are getting into ahead of time.

So far so good? Great. Now its time to check out the amenities. Is there a nice backyard with a deck on which to sip cool ones ? If you are lucky enough to afford a car, is there a place to park the heap? Does it cost extra? How about laundry? A-AConsider what the neighbours and the neighbourhood is like. If the place is in one of those high rise apartment buildings, you might want to hang out for a bit and do some careful listening. If it seems that there are divorce proceedings under way in the apartment to the North, kids training for some sort of Bruce Lee remake to the South, Rock 'N Roll deadheads with stereos blaring to the West and some sort of amateur musician torturing his clarinet to the East, it may be time to consider other accommodations. Be sure to do your listening on a Sunday afternoon when everyone is home and noise levels are likely to be at a peak.

Don't forget to consider alternatives beyond the high rise apartment building. Sometimes part of a duplexed house can provide a very decent lifestyle. Find one in a nice neighbourhood with reasonable people living in the other half and you are all set. If you live in one of those cosmopolitan cities with a heavy urban renewal program, you might even be able to get a deal on some sort of converted warehouse and make like some sort of cool Richard Gere type.

Make sure to check which bills you will be responsible for and figure that into your affordability calculations. Make sure all roommates have signed one lease, so that if one moves out, you are not stuck with the financial responsibility.

Anything goes. I recall living in a place we called The Cave. The owner was a friend of my roommate to be. He was a sax player in a bar band and owned a tiny house with an unfinished basement. In May, (like a total buffoon) I agreed to rent what looked like the cave they bricked Fortunato into as he cried out for mercy. According to the sax player/landlord/carpenter, while it didn't look like much now, by August, he promised that the mirrored tiles would pick up the sunlight from the new windows and gently dust it onto the granite columns...

...Returning in August from a summer job out of town, I found essentially the same basement that I had viewed in May. A cascade of assurances were buttressed with a tide of promises, but very little construction. In the end, I pitched in and did much of the drywall, wiring, plumbing and flooring. As the November snow began to fly, I even had an entrance door to cover the gaping hole left by the jackhammer that cleared an opening in October. Although I lived most of my first term in a construction zone, the first couple months were free and I have since saved thousands of dollars by putting to use my new found renovation skills. What the hell!

Then there was the guy at my school who lived in the library. He would slink in just before closing and hide up in the book stacks on Greek Mythology where he had hidden his sleeping bag, clothing supply and a muffled alarm clock. In the morning, he would head down to the university gym for a shower and a shave and off to class. Your school may have motion detectors in the library to guard against this technique, but for those cash-strapped months it may be a thought...

Back to finding your new place. Try to look at a few places before you commit. Few things can wrench your guts as badly as buyer's remorse. If you grab the place you are looking at right now and a friend invites you over to the spotless pad with the Jacuzzi and sun deck for which she pays $100.00 less per month, how will you feel? If you look at only two places, you can at least feel smug about the fact that some poor shlep will get stuck with that other place that you so wisely turned down.

Signing Up

With your mind made up, its time to sign. Don't panic. Most landlords will use a standard form lease. In North America, in landlord vs tenant matters the tenant generally carries the upper hand. If you are in doubt, look up the appropriate government agency that deals with tenant rights. Give them a call before you commit to anything that seems fishy. Give the lease a good read through and ask about anything that doesn't seem reasonable. Usually the deal is fairly straightforward. Generally, the landlord will want first and last months rent up front, so that if you skip out at any time, she has the next month's rent covered to pay the mortgage while she searches for a new tenant. Damage deposits (money paid up front to insure against potential damages) may not be legal, so check before paying one. Some landlords used to prorate rent to students since they tend to skip out and not pay rent through the summer months. That too, is usually illegal.

With your contract signed, its usually a matter of handing over first and last months rent, getting the keys and voila. Make sure that you get day and nighttime phone numbers for your landlord as well. Is there someone else that you can call in the case of an emergency? Also, find out how to control the heat and the air conditioning. Be sure to get receipts for your first and last months rent and for the months in between. You might be able to claim these amounts on your income tax. Finally, it is imperative that you call an insurance company to get a tenant's package on your new place to protect you in case of fire, flooding or theft. The hundred bucks a year or so is worth the peace of mind since, in most cases, the landlord is not responsible should the pipes burst and soak all your goodies.

Moving Day

If you are like most students, moving should be a snap. Be careful with the stereo, throw the rest of the stuff in garbage bags, recruit a half dozen of the largest people you know (or can meet in time before the move) and presto!

To make life easier during the move, here are a few more tips: Before the move, scour local liquor and grocery stores for good boxes. Buy yourself a roll of packing tape and a heavy felt tip marker. Load the boxes with items that are destined for a common room. Seal them with your new roll of packing tape and, you guessed it, write the detailed contents and the destination room on the outside of the box with that new marker of yours. When your buddies come, they will know exactly where to take everything. All you have to do is bum a truck from someone, buy a case of beer and order the pizza.

Most importantly, before you move out of your parent's house be sure to squirrel away any items that they may have that would prove useful in your new abode. In particular, look for blenders (great for making Margaritas and Daiquiris), kitchen items (in case you plan on eating anything during the next three years), blankets, artwork, rugs, furniture (couches made out of empty beer cases and milk crates can look a touch stark after a while) and pretty well anything else you can manage to cart away. Most parents have a strong inclination to shower you with all manner of goodies when you leave their nest. If your parents seem to lack this reflex and simply wave goodbye, you may have to do some work to cultivate it in them.

Whatever happens, do not turn anything down. Even if you can't use it or wouldn't be caught dead wearing it, you might be able to sell it to raise some cash or burn it to help keep your place cozy in the winter.

Problems, What Problems?

So you have been happily living in your new place for a month or two when something happens. What happens? Who knows? It could be anything, but it is a problem if it comes up and you don't know what to do about it. First of all, don't panic. Don't worry about it either. Think of all the times that you have agonized over something and then it never happened. Right? With a clear, relaxed mind and the handy little house problem guide that follows, you will be ready for anything.

Fry an egg on the window sill?

Let me guess. It is the summer, you are attending the University of Amarillo and the air conditioner that is supposed to keep the fish bowl from boiling over, isn't. A scorpion just strolled by and fainted. Apparently heat prostration. What to do?

First, determine if the place has an air conditioner. Any big grey boxes poking their nose out the window? How about a big grey box outside somewhere with hoses that head into the house? No? Well you have no air conditioner and the landlord lied.

If you have one of those room air conditioners, first check to ensure that it is plugged in. Next, try setting the temperature to "coldest" and turning the thing on. If it runs, but doesn't spit out cold air, the unit needs to be serviced. Call your landlord or take the thing in to a service centre.

If you throw the switch and you get nothing, you have a blown fuse. Take a flashlight and find the fuse box for the house (a large grey metal box screwed in to the wall with a hinged door on the front). They are usually in the basement somewhere or hidden in a closet. Pull the door open and you should see a number of round glass fuses. Shine your flashlight on them. Most should look shiny and clean inside the glass, but you may have one that looks like all hell has broken loose inside. Unscrew the little sucker and take it to a hardware store (or even a corner variety store) and ask the nice clerk for one just like it. Go for broke get a spare one for next time. Walk your new fuse home, screw it in and try the A/C out one more time. Hopefully that should do it. Make sure nothing else is plugged in to the same circuit, or the fuse may blow again.

If you have central air conditioning (big grey box outside somewhere) you will have a control for it somewhere within your apartment or house. It's a little beige box on the wall somewhere with some numbers on it. Is there a little switch on it somewhere that says Heat Off Cool? If it isn't switched to Cool, it may be as simple as that. Next, trying setting the temperature to a lower setting (try 20°C or 70°F). Ahh, the whoosh of cool air throughout your home. Still no luck? Best to call the landlord.

Cat Frozen In His Tracks?

Don't tell me. Let me guess. You have been reading the problems of the student at U of Amarillo and you are green with envy. Make that blue with envy. With slurred speech and your body restricting blood flow to the extremities to ensure warmth of your vital organs, you strain your numb fingers to turn these pages in search of warmth. Strain no more.

To begin, try to figure out what heats the place. Do you have large metal finned things in each of the rooms? They are radiators. With a little coaxing, we should be able to get some heat out of them. Or perhaps you have grates on the walls or floors which are supposed to spew forth warm air. They are part of a forced air system. You can't do much with these yourself other than adjust the thermostat. Or you may have long skinny beige metal things that run along the floorboards. These are electric baseboard heaters. I will have to deal with you different types one at a time.

About Radiators

OK. First you radiator people. Scoot around the place and see if your radiators are hot or warm. Are they cold? Are they all cold? If some are good and warm and some are cold, you will have to bleed any that are cold. Ah, you don't like bloodshed or you are a conscientious objector? No problem. First, make sure that the valve at the bottom of the radiator on the pipes is open. Try turning it counter-clockwise to open it. If it was closed (all the way counter clockwise), that might have been your problem right there. Next, somewhere near the top of the radiator there will be a small knob. Put a glass under the knob and loosen it (counter-clockwise). It should hiss for a while. Let it hiss as long as it likes. When it is through hissing, you will see a few drops of water come out. Tighten the knob back up and the radiator (and you) will be warm shortly. Some of these bleed valves will need to be loosened with a screwdriver. Whatever you do, be gentle so that you don't start the thing leaking.

If all of your radiators are cold, or if you are one of those forced air people that I described earlier, head to the thermostat on the wall (probably a little beige box on the wall in the living or dining room). There should be a little switch on the side that says Heat Off Cool. Switch the thing to Heat and turn the setting up to 70°F or 20°C. Give it a minute and see if you feel any signs of warmth. If you are warm, great. Otherwise, call your landlord.

About Baseboard Heaters

Ah, you baseboard people are still out there and shivering, aren't t t tttt ttt yyyy ooouuu? Take a look at one of those long skinny beige things attached to the wall just above the floor. Is there a round knob on it that looks like it might control the heat coming out of it? It does. Try turning it clockwise to see if it starts spitting out some heat. No luck? Call the landlord. No knob on the heater? Is there one on a wall in the room somewhere? Maybe hidden behind a bookcase or a plant. If you find one, try setting it higher. If you can't find it, call the landlord. They are never around when you need them. Who said that?

And Then, About Water – Flooding

You have woken up or come home to discover the place awash in water. Omigod. Is the water still flowing? If it is winter time, it was probably a pipe that burst. Alternately, a sink or tub has overflowed. If so, and you know where the main water valve is (a good thing to know) for your house or apartment, go shut it off. If the water is from a sprinkler system, call the fire department if it isn't obvious that they have already been there. Otherwise, it could be a backed up sewer or a leaky basement. Move to higher ground taking with you anything of consequence that needs to stay dry. Call the landlord for help.

Plugged sinks?

You can brush your teeth in the sink, head off to school, get some lunch, enjoy a game of squash and make it home before the sink drains? No problem. If you are mechanically inclined, you can take apart that strange curved pipe underneath the sink (the "P trap") and clean it out. Be forewarned. Lurking within that trap is the slimiest, ugliest, grossest little beastie you have ever seen in your life. Never mind Ghost Busters and old Stephen King movies. THIS STUFF IS GROSS. Generally it is a mixture of hair, partially decomposed food, slime, goo and miscellaneous smelly black stuff.

If I have twinged your curiosity and you own a monkey wrench, read on. Get a bucket under the P trap and affix your wrench to one of the large nuts on the pipe. Loosen the nut (counter clockwise), while bracing the pipe with your free hand. Be gentle. With the one nut loosened off, undo the other one. With the nuts taken off, pull the trap down. Ssssloosh. Ugh. Did the trap beastie come out? I know. What a stench. I warned you. Use a screwdriver or a coat hanger to poke out the remaining sludge and then reassemble the works. Run some water and check for leaks.

Don't have the nerve, the wrench or the mechanical skill? Have a peek under the sink at the pipes. If they are old and ugly, they are cast iron. Shiny orange metal? They are copper. Black plastic? These are ABS plastic pipes. Go to the hardware store, tell 'em what kind of pipes you have and get some drain cleaner. Be careful with this stuff. Read the directions carefully and be sure to wear whatever protective gear they recommend. Pour the stuff down the drain and flush with water as the directions outline. Still have problems? Back to the landlord. Wherever he or she is.

Plugged toilets?

You've been there yourself. You are out on a heavy date with this awesome vision or dreamy hunk and you head back for a nightcap. Suddenly, you feel this irrepressible urge to go to the bathroom. You politely inquire as to its whereabouts, dash in and release Tuesday's dinner. Then the panic strikes. You press the lever hoping for a powerful flush to swoosh away all of the evils that you have left there, but little happens. All the little goodies float around aimlessly in the bowl. A second flush yields few additional results. Time ticks on. Your dreamboat calls out from the living room to see if you are OK. You feel the heat rise up in your cheeks...

Unplugging a toilet is not a pleasant affair, but it is generally straightforward. If it is plugged and continuing to fill up, locate the shiny chrome valve on the water inlet pipe near the wall and shut it off (clockwise). Now take a toilet plunger and place it over the large hole in the bowl of the toilet and give it a half dozen good thrusts. Release. Any action? Try smearing a little Vaseline around the edge of the plunger to give it a better seal, then another few good plunges. That should do it. Keep repeating the process until it flushes properly. If you are still out of luck, you are going to have to fess up to your date. If the embarassment is just too much, try sliding out the bathroom window. Figure out an excuse to tell your date later.

A Visit From Mickey

If the tale (tail?) at the beginning of this chapter sounds at all familiar and you have quickly flipped to this section, don't despair. It is very difficult to eliminate mice completely, but with a little work, you can keep them under control.

Mice are incredibly frisky little creatures. They can scale brick walls, crawl through holes the size of a dime and eat any type of food, most building materials and pretty well anything they can get their teeny paws on. The good news is they are generally more afraid of you than you are of them and are quickly frightened by your movements. They are, for example, not very likely to curl up in bed with you.

There are basically two things that you can do. One is to leave out mouse poison, which usually consists of particles like bird seed that are impregnated with anti-coagulants so that the mice haemorrhage internally and die. Nice huh? The problem is that you have absolutely no idea where they are going to die. I used to use this method until one day I stepped out of bed with my bare feet. Nothing is grosser.

Bringing us to the second option. Get yourself two or three of the good, old-fashioned, wooden mouse traps. No one has built them better. Put them wherever you see those miniature 'raisins' around the house. Also, best to put them somewhere out of immediate sight and somewhere that you won't step on them (again, advice from personal experience). You might consider behind the fridge, the TV or the stereo. Get yourself a jar of peanut butter and prepare to load.

Now, I realize that many of you are questioning my use of peanut butter, since every three year old kid knows that mice eat cheese. I can't explain it, really, but peanut butter has always worked well for me. If you are a traditionalist, by all means, use cheese. Pull the wire bale back (against the effort of the spring) and pinch it against the wood using your thumb and forefinger. With the other hand, use a knife to smear a tiny dollop of peanut butter on the little metal flap. Work it right into the hole on the flap so that Mickey has to get his nose right in there. Now flip the straight metal wire over the bale that you are holding back and under the lip on the flap with the peanut butter on it. Change your grip to the sides of the wood base (out of harm's way) and *carefully* set the trap down on its destination. Check your trap lines every day.

Aha! I can tell by that smug look on your face that you have been out checking your trap lines and you are gloating with success. Victory is sweet. The squeamish among you may be wondering how to gracefully remove this corpse without having to actually touch it. You are reading the right book, my friend.

Pick the trap up by the sides once again and hold the whole works (mouse, trap and remaining peanut butter) over a garbage can. Reaching around the mouse, pull back the bail wire just as you did when you were loading the trap. Give the whole thing a vigorous shaking and the mouse should dislodge nicely. Is your mouse hanging on? Sometimes the metal bale will put a nasty kink in their little necks. Give the trap another good shake or two. I have never seen a mouse that wouldn't let go eventually. Worst case, have a friend give the mouse a good prod with a blunt instrument while you hold back the bale. Be sure to reload you trap and wash your hands when you are done.

Squeamish and/or rich? Throw the whole works out and buy another trap.

You may find that you score a whole herd of mice in the first week. One of the great truths of life is that no one has just one mouse. Hopefully, things will taper off and you will be down to just a trickle over the long haul. Also, be sure to keep your kitchen clean and avoid leaving food lying around the house. That includes all of you who keep a bag of Nacho flavoured Cheese Doritos by your bed. Back in the kitchen, trying storing your food in the cabinets above the sink and keep pots, pans and the like in the lower cupboards.

Over time, you will come to enjoy the thrill of the hunt and the incredible feeling of elation that comes from a successful session of trapping. While the temptation may be there to save and cure the little pelts, I would suggest that your Davey Crocket time be more productively spent.

Evil Roommates.

It is for good reason that this section lies between the one on mice and the one on cockroaches.

Roommates that have, shall we say, less than the ideal chemistry, can make for a miserable existence. Begin by picking them carefully. One of the biggest sore points tends to be the level of cleanliness.

Few things can be as aggravating as cleaning up after a slob. If you are the one doing endless piles of other people's dishes, taking out the garbage and picking the underwear off the fridge, you can sympathize. Keep in mind that with three roommates, each will claim to be doing most of the cleaning. The mathematical proof of this is a little complex, but trust me. By the time you get to second year algebra, you will understand that it is not possible to have three people, each of whom does *all* the cleaning.

Try to see the places that your potential roommates live in now. History is still the best predictor of future performance.

If you have roommates that are brutal, try to have a household meeting to reason with them. Get your feelings out early, before they build up inside of you and you do a Stephen King number on them. If no amount of reason, discussion, coercion or negotiation will get them to straighten up their act, you will have to get rid of them to preserve your sanity.

Try foisting them off on an enemy of the opposite sex, in the hopes that they will move in together. Band together with the good roommates to try and terrorize them out. Leave a half pound of ripe Limburger Cheese under their bed. Change the locks. Do what it takes. Above all, remember that roommates, like parents, must be carefully chosen to avoid a lifetime of problems.

La Cucaracha?

Did it scurry across the tub? Leap out of your jar of flour? Dart out of the baseboards? Cockroaches are ugly little pests and they can get into almost anything, since they don't have that dime-sized hole restriction that so severely handicaps mice from invading your entire home.

Once again, it's time to visit your friendly hardware store to check out the selection of sprays and potions that you can spread around to rid yourself of these beasts. They seem to enjoy damp and dirty climates, so try to keep your bathroom and kitchen clean and dry. if they are really persistent, talk to your landlord about having the place sprayed by the nice men in the white overalls with the big tanks strapped to their backs.

Legal problems

For whatever reason, things have gone grossly awry. Your roommates have skipped out on you without leaving rent money. A big bash caused an uninvited soul, overcome with youthful excess, to bash his head through the drywall in the hallway. Someone left the bathtub running and it overflowed into the kitchen.

Whatever happened, happened. The point is, you now have a landlord breathing down your neck and muttering all kinds of things about paying for damages, lawsuits and the like. What to do?

First of all keep your cool. These things always turn out to be much tamer than you originally expected. Lawsuits seldom materialize and time remains the best healer of all ills. Remember too, that lawsuits are an expensive business for both sides. The landlord knows that launching a lawsuit is a several thousand dollar proposition and those kinds of costs represent several times the maximum amount that she is likely to get out of you, a broke student. Shrug off the lawsuit and present a positive helpful image. Try to reason. Is there something that you can do to help set things right? A landlord is unlikely to hold your feet to the fire if there is a feeling that you are at least trying to be helpful. A little *genuine* remorse helps too.

If things remain sticky, check the government pages of the phone book for the tenant rights groups. A few phone calls should put you in touch with the right department. Usually there is some sort of organization that will help you out. You will also find that the landlord and tenant laws found in Canada and the United States (they may be one country by the time you read this) heavily favour the tenant. If things make it as far as the court room, you likely have nothing to worry about.

Remember that your new student hovel will be the place that will house not only you, but all of your student memories. Choose it with care, but not too much care. A few small disasters will make for good stories in later years.

4 THE PAPER STORM
– birth of a filing cabinet

Missing Stuff Scenario #1

You arrive home from school, starving to death. Rummaging through the cupboard you find only one box of noodle dinner left. The package was opened, but all of the little noodles seemed to be present and accounted for, so you dumped the whole works into the pot. When everything is boiled and ready to go, you pour in some milk and add the... No sauce mix.

Missing Stuff Scenario #2

You had put off doing your part of the cost accounting assignment for far too long. To appease your panic stricken group, you had told them that you were just putting the finishing touches on it. With the group meeting tomorrow morning at 8:00, it was going to be one busy night. But when you got home your roommate was watching the 49'ers playing the Raiders and you figured that your assignment could hold out for the first half. The NFL led to Wheel of Fortune and then Jeopardy, sucking you in for several extra hours as often happens while one is positioned in front of that powerful Time Vacuum. (Is that why they call it TV?) By the time Alex had asked the final question under Geography, it was 10:00 PM. You arrived up at your desk and shuffled through your papers to find your copy of the assignment outline that... wasn't there.

Missing Stuff Scenario #3

Hard to believe, but your graduation had finally arrived. You had spent most of the day celebrating at the beach with the gang and had cut it a little close to get home in time to get changed for the graduation ceremony. While you were excited about finally getting it all over with, the idea of donning the corporate duds was less than appealing. With your best suit enhancing the lines of your physique, the toothpaste residue still in your mouth, twenty seven minutes until the start of the ceremony, a carload of relatives waiting and dad honking the car horn outside, you tear apart your room in search of your dress shoes that... aren't there.

Let's face it. We all lose stuff from time to time. Enough said. We can all relate to the problem. Before getting to some solutions, lets pause for a moment to better understand the reasons that our essentials go AWOL.

The Laws of Disappearing Articles

The Law of Usefulness

Useless things do not get lost. For a thing to be lost, there must be someone in pursuit of it. It's a bit like a tree falling in the forest. Given that it is a useful thing, odds are it's useful to someone else as well as you and they have taken it.

The Law of Vanishing Returns

If someone borrows your stuff, they probably had a powerful need for it. Enough to overcome their need to ask you for yours. Enough for them to do a search of their place to see if they have one. But now, with yours securely borrowed and in place, allowing them to carry on with their business and save the parking, hassle, cost and aggravation of buying their own and giving you back yours, they just carry on with it. When you need it back it's gone. Who borrowed it? Who knows?

The Law of Entropy

China vases don't gather up their pieces from the floor, refill themselves with water and carefully arranged flowers. Bicycle rims do not take time out to straighten themselves after a steep curb encounter. A full beer left on the patio in August will not re-chill itself and seek out fresh bubbles. And your economics notes will not staple themselves together or sort themselves into chronological order in a file folder just before you begin to study for the final.

Getting Organized

OK. So now we know what a pain it is to lose stuff and we know how it might happen. How do we stow it so that we can find it when we need it, you ask?

First, we need to get some organizing gear. For just a few bucks, you can get everything that you will need to amass all of your school notes, gas bills, stereo warranties, grade reports and term papers. In fact, we will build you a complete system so that, with only five minutes of organizing time each day, you will be able to locate any relevant piece of paper that you will need to find during the entire school year. Noodle dinner sauce mix, assignment outlines or dress shoes? You are on your own.

Daily Notes

What are you supposed to do with 'em after you write all of the stuff down? How do you know where one day ends and the next begins? What if you lose the one page that you really need?

Begin by getting yourself one of those plastic clipboards with the flap that closes over the paper. Stock the thing up with three hole binder paper at the start of each day. As you go to each class, write the course code at the top of each page as well as the date. Number each page as you go, and be sure to use the back of each page to help keep the planet green. Next class? Get out a fresh piece of paper and put the new course code at the top. Stow your completed notes in the handy pouch. Simple.

End of Day Logistics

Beauty. Lots of great notes. Put them in order of page numbers and subjects. Staple together each complete day's worth of notes so that you don't lose that one critical page. But where do they go?

In your new filing cabinet.

I know. You don't see yourself as the filing cabinet type. What next, a station wagon and some brown oxfords? Ya gotta do what ya gotta do. Start with a two drawer and work your way up. Be sure to ask for all the fixin's so that you can use hanging file folders like the real pros. If the guy at the stationary store indicates a lack of understanding of what you mean by 'you know, a filing cabinet with all the fixins', just show his manager this picture:

She'll get you the right one.

Wondering whether these cabinets are made of platinum? Expensive little suckers aren't they? Too pricey? See if the nice people at the stationary store have any of those cardboard file folder holder boxes. Or you might be able to hunt down a good used metal cabinet. They come in useful in later life when you need to seek out the guarantee for the lawn mower, or you want to track your spouse's clothing bills from the previous year for your annual variance analysis.

While the nice manager is helping you, get a whole wack of file folders and hanging folders to keep everything nice and straight. If you are a real organization buff, pick up a roll of those little file folder stickers as well. What the hell.

When you get home, put the whole works together. As usual, they probably hosed you and you are missing a screw or something. The whole cabinet feels like a piece of junk right? Until the Japanese get into building filing cabinets, there's not much we can do.

Oops. You need a hacksaw to cut the little gizmo that holds the hanging files, or a screwdriver to bolt the whole works together? Check around your place. No luck? See if you can borrow one from a neighbour. Give it back when you are done.

Set up one hanging file for each subject using the little tabs provided (did you forget the tabs?) and then set up file folders for each subject – one for notes, and one for each of term papers, lab notes, textbook notes, assignments, course outlines, old exams or whatever. Put all file folders for each subject into the hanging file that you have set up for it. Colour coding can be helpful too.

Dynamite.

No more lost notes for you. At the end of each day, in go the stapled notes du jour and you are all set. Exam time? Cake. just grab all the file folders for the subject and the textbook and head off to the library (no fridge, no TV, no telephone).

Bills, Various, Miscellaneous and Sundry Papers

Your aunt sent you a great article. Your picture is in the paper for winning the submarine eating contest. Your new bike lock comes with a warranty. You scribble down a great business idea. A summer employer writes you a letter of recommendation. You clip out a Herman cartoon.

Where do you file all this stuff? And how come you keep accumulating more of it?

Easy. The top drawer of your cabinet should be large enough to hold a full year's worth of school notes. Use the bottom drawer for everything else. Set up a hanging file for bills, one for guarantees, another for ideas, articles, warranties, memorabilia and so on. For each major category, use a hanging file and for each minor category, use a file folder. For bills, you might set up a hanging file called Bills and then have a file folder for each type: Electricity, Gas, Water, etc. Store all the bills in chronological order in each file, so that if you have to refer back, they are easy to find.

Still have some effects that defy a logical filing system? How about some stuff that doesn't deserve a hanging file of its own, but doesn't fit into any of your pre-established sub groups? Pitch it out. How important can it be if it doesn't fit into a pre-established sub group?

For non school stuff, you might try getting yourself one of those plastic accordion files. They are handy to get in and out of, very portable and a whole bunch cheaper than another filing cabinet.

Bills

Have you ever had a bill buried under other paperwork and forgot to pay it? What kind of a stupid question is that? Who hasn't? It was a convenient excuse and worked pretty well until the electric company got wise and plunged your place into darkness, right?

Enough fun and games. The real question is where do you stash your bills during the time that you receive them and up until you mail them a couple of weeks after the date you wrote on the cheque? Back dating the envelope using the postage meter from Mom's office too, are you? Sly dog.

When you get them, rip them open to survey the damage. Get yourself some sort of makeshift IN/OUT tray just like the big shooters have. Stack the bills up on the IN tray in the order that they are due. As new ones come in, slip them into the proper chronological sequence. Every couple of days, under low lighting and with no one else around, gingerly peek at the top bill to see if it is due yet. Write a cheque as late as you dare, put it in the return envelope with the remittance slip, write the amount paid on your receipt and file it in your Bill Hanging File Main Group in proper chronological order, toss the completed envelope in your OUT tray for mailing the next day. Keep filing the new bills and mailing the old ones from the top of the pile. Presto. The lights stay on, the water stays hot and you don't get evicted.

Laundry

Laundry? OK, maybe laundry shouldn't fit in here, but it didn't fit into any of the other major sub groups that I had already set up. I have some good tips that shouldn't be wasted and this seemed like a good spot to fit them in. Besides, laundry is like anything else: you get the best results when you are organized.

So you come home late, peel off your clothes to jump into bed and what are you supposed to do with them? The simple thing is to toss your gauchies on the floor and test your jump shot with your socks. This approach is functional, but it probably annoys the hell out of your roommates.

Enter the laundry basket. A common spot to squirrel away all of your wayward clothes until you can help them on their path to the washing machine. If you get yourself a basket that is rigid, you will be able to toss your clothes in from across the room. This ease of access will make it more likely for you to actually use the thing.

A large cloth bag, on the other hand facilitates toting your dirty duds off to the laundromat. I will leave this important decision up to you. As a big executive you will one day find that you knock off such weighty decisions almost intuitively, but for now, take your time and get the laundry bag or basket that best suits your needs.

Every school has those nerds who will carefully separate out their whites from their coloureds, using different wash temperatures and detergents for each. These people should be in the washers with their carefully sorted laundry. By the time I graduated, however, I do have to admit that virtually all of my clothes had converged on a single colour. It was kind of a muted purplish-grey, yet another confirmation of the existence of our friend Entropy – warming beer, greying T-shirts and creating a mess in the kitchen.

The solution, I later learned, is to get two laundry repositories – one for anything close to white and one for darker colours. Take the two containers to the laundromat and wash the loads separately.

Here's the only thing that you have to know: Wash your whites in hot water and your coloureds in warm water. Simple as that. If you are still worried about looking a touch anal retentive with all of this sorting and separating, just take one load to get washed at a time. So you happened to have only white laundry that week. So who's askin' anyway? I used to have a roommate who had three baskets, one for whites, one for coloureds and one for dry cleaning. I laughed at him up until last year, when I raised him one basket to stow my spare change in. If you have any ideas fora fifth basket, please write and let me know.

Do we need to bother with all this anti static stuff for the dryer? Looks a bit wimpy doesn't it? I mean, who isn't strong enough to pull their clothes apart?. Besides, if you turn out the lights while you separate the charged laundry, you can have your own personal lightning storm. On the other hand, how long will it take to live down strolling around on campus with a sock stuck to your back? Get some of those little sheets for the dryer. The answer to your next question is no, you can't reuse those little sheets or use ones that you found discarded in the laundromat. The manufacturers are on to that game. Planned obsolescence.

Like employing birth control devices every other time, overloading your washer is false economy. Fill the clothes to the top of the vanes on the white thing that sticks up in the middle. Don't use cheap detergent. Its cliche as all get out, but Tide really does seem to get clothes clean.

Organizing Your Food

Oh yeah. One more thing. How do you organize your food? If you live on your own, you can pretty well jam in it your cupboards any way you can. Try to keep the good stuff tucked in behind the oatmeal, soup and broccoli. Otherwise you will have a great dinner of Oreo's, Sour Cream and Chive crackers and Tin Roof Ice cream and have to tough it out the rest of the week on tofu, bean sprouts and tomatoes.

If you have a roommate, the dynamics change dramatically. Hide all of the good stuff under your bed. To discourage nibbling from the enemy camp, mark the current levels of your stuff on the outside of the container with an ultraviolet marker. Consider the use of surveillance cameras throughout the kitchen. Above all go for revenge and vindication with escalating punitive damages. She steals an Oreo, you polish off her ice cream. He eats a couple of your Chipits, wipe out his entire cracker reserves. Somebody gets into your chips, eat their steaks. As Sean Connery said, "That's the Chicago way".

Organize your papers, sort your laundry, guard your food. You'll make it through.

5 POST PROCRASTINATING – rushin' student time management

Years later. I still have the nightmare.

I am back in engineering school. In the sunny days of September, I am busy purchasing text books, racing from class to class, meeting classmates and grasping to understand what each new course is all about. But with six subjects competing for my time, days blur into weeks, fade to months and a whole term nearly slips by. Exams and assignments materialize, are submitted and the results displayed back all too graphically. Friendships grow, romances wax and wane, jeans fade and grunge accumulates on the shelves of my refrigerator. The end of the term nears.

The scramble to get the last bits of work done. Clear the decks for the finals. Old exams are passed around and studied with intensity. Joining the gang in the cafeteria, the discussion turns to that inevitable exam schedule. Bits of the talk whirl around in my mind, inciting evil, dreading sense of déjà vu. An unbearable pressure overcomes me. My heart pounds in my ears.

Why do the course materials being discussed bring back only fogged memories? The truth begins to dawn. The exams begin ***this*** *week, not next. What they are discussing starts* ***in one hour***. *I haven't been to any of the lectures except the first two back in September. I don't even know why I didn't go. How could I plum forget about an entire course for a whole term?*

I snatch a text book and desperately flip through the pages hoping it will somehow seep in. But it all swirls in a vortex devoid of meaning. My mind convulses, zooming in and out at a dizzying pace. My fear is gripping, my year is destroyed, my future has vaporized.

I wake up.

Daily planners

Poor time management can leave us with a constant feeling of uncertainty that burgeons into nightmares like this one. More specifically, we really need to manage the events in our lives, time will take care of itself. The best place to begin is with a daily planner to keep track of pub nights, dates, cafeteria specials and yes, even exam schedules.

Step one is to go out and buy yourself a good planner. No need to get too fancy. Don't spend a lot of money for one that provides international time zones when the only phone calls you make are to arrange dates and you seldom carry on romances across state or provincial boundaries. Similarly, a wine chilling chart is a touch redundant if your principal apéritif is a can of Coors Light.

Look for a calendar that gives ample room for each day and has some blank pages in the front to allow room for your goals and empty sections in the back where you can record little pearls of wisdom as they materialize in your cranium. Pick one large enough for some details, but small enough that you will always keep it with you. Take your new book home and get it set up.

Goals

They may be boring and cliché, but they are essential. What and by when. The four minute mile was not eclipsed by Roger Bannister ambling to the corner store for a quart of butter brickle and then settling in front of the TV to watch Jetson reruns. Einstein did not develop his theory of relativity while gabbing with friends on the phone, scratching his gut and idly flipping over cards in a game of solitaire.

Begin your new journey of time mastery by writing out what it is that you hope to accomplish this term. To aid in this exercise, use the following categories as examples to ensure that you are covering all goal areas that are relevant to you.

Scholastic – What grades do you hope to accomplish in each subject? Are you aiming for top quartile overall? Dean's List? A pass?

Physical – Fifty lengths of the pool by the end of term? A six minute mile? A two hundred pound bench press?

Spiritual – What are you going to read or study that will help you to become a more worthwhile person? An excellent start is Scott Peck's *The Road Less Travelled*. Get involved in yourself beyond passing the next exam. Where better to invest?

Charitable – What activities will you accomplish this term to help others who are less fortunate than you? Are there campus groups that you can involve yourself in?

When you have your goals refined, write them down in the first page of your time calendar. Tough to do isn't it? What if someone sees your goals? Worse still, what if they are never realised? What if you don't have the time to write down your goals? Perhaps they are not yet clear. Take a stab. If people see them, they will respect your organization skills and will wish that they had the goods to write theirs down as well. Demand nothing of yourself and you will receive it.

Whoa. What are you doing reading onto the next paragraph without writing down your goals in the front of your time calendar? Take five minutes and get it done. Then you can read on.

Schedule Everything

Take another five minutes and gather all of your course outlines your class timetable and your time calendar. Cart the whole works down to your couch, relax in front of the TV and tune in to an old Star Trek rerun. As the crew of the Starship Enterprise explores unknown galaxies and boldly goes where no man has gone before, you will be busy plugging all of your labs, lectures, tutorials, assignment due dates and exams into your calendar for the entire term. By the time credits roll up the screen, the Klingons will be safely back in control, Lt. O'Hura will have a secured supply of dilithium crystals and you will be safely in control of the major events of the term.

The next day while you are waiting at Student Health Services to have that suspicious itch in the unmentionable spot checked out, pull out your time calendar and block out your exercise time slots for the term. I know. Its boring and repetitive. But what else would you be doing sitting in the waiting room for all this time? Reading last year's Time Magazines? Checking out the other patients to guess what they have? Also take a moment to schedule in some time each day to get some work done on specific assignments and review the lecture materials from each day.

What? No Time Left?

As you schedule in time for lectures, exercise, assignment work and social events, be sure to leave some buffer zones where you will have a chance to smell the roses. Don't get yourself so constrained that you can't spend a moment chatting with a friend or lingering over a frozen yogurt.

Pulling the Day Together

The night before

Each night take fifteen minutes to go through your calendar for the next day. Did you get all of today's list done? If not, take a moment to determine its priority. Is it necessary to do at all? Forget it. Can it live for a week? Schedule it in to an open spot next week.

What do you need to do to prepare for tomorrow? Assemble the books and papers that you will need for the next day and get them ready in your knapsack (OK, you biz students, your briefcase). Do a look ahead for the next month as well. Have you scheduled time in to work on some Tupcoming assignments? Are midterm exams approaching? Don't use a 'To Do' list. Schedule everything into a particular time slot. As soon as it is all committed to paper, you will find a tremendous drop in your anxiety level.

Through the day

As you proceed through the day, use the blank back pages to jot down ideas as you get them and schedule in any new events or commitments as they occur during the day. Include social and athletic events and newly arranged romantic outings.

Check off those items that are completed through the day, including lectures that you attended and exercise regimens that you had the discipline to follow through with. The sense of accomplishment from reaching your goals for the day leads to a tremendous feeling of self worth.

At lunch time, have a look to see how the day is shaping up. Are you on track with your events for the day? Has anything happened so far that will need an entry for a subsequent day? Is there anything that needs to be done prior to the events of the afternoon?

An ideal time to work in some exercise is after your last class of the day. A fiery game of squash, a couple dozen laps of the pool or an invigorating jog around campus is a great way to clear out your mind and provide yourself with the second wind that you will need to power your way through the evening.

When you arrive back at home, set aside half an hour to gather and sort your lecture notes and staple the related notes from each lecture together. Before filing them away in their proper resting places, take a minute and read through them for a quick refresher course. If anything is missing or there are sections that you don't understand, check the textbook or make a note in your calendar to bring it up with a buddy the next day at school. As you go through your notes, watch for work that your professor has assigned. Estimate the time that it will take to complete and when it will need to be done by. Take a second and schedule it straight into your calendar. No need to worry about it any more.

And into the evening

With today safely organized, scheduled and reviewed, it's time to take a dinner break before getting tonight's projects completed. Flip to 'Beyond the Care Package' and cook up the selection of your choice. Know what time your dinner break ends, though, otherwise it will stretch to 10:30. When you have polished off the last morsel, get back to your desk and get at it. But first, DO THE DISHES. You won't be able to concentrate properly knowing that an ugly slimy scrunge is slowly entrenching itself over all of your dishes into that crusty coating that will take hours to remove.

Back to your desk to tackle this evening's assignments. Take a look at what you have recorded in your calendar for tonight. Which is the most urgent item that will most affect your grades for the year? *Tackle it first.* If you begin with the task that you would prefer to do, you will drag it out until there is no time left to tackle the one that you needed to do that night.

Always ask yourself the question "Is what I am doing right now the most important thing that I could be doing at this time to help me meet my goals?" If the answer is no, move on to what you should be doing. Don't do tasks just for the sake of crossing them off the list. There is a priority to most things.

When you have completed your assignment or project work for the night, cross the items off and then take a moment to review your goals for the term. Were you able to make progress toward all of your goals today? What should you add to tomorrow's schedule to get you back on track?

With today all sorted out, clear all of the left over paper work off your desk. "The Paper Storm" told you where to put everything, so there's no excuse for not having a clean desk at the end of the day.

And thinking of tomorrow

Once again its time to take a few moments to have a look at tomorrow's schedule. Does it prepare you for upcoming assignments? Do you have some buffer time scheduled? Time for social events and fun? Time to review your notes from the day? With everything down in your calendar, your desk cleared off and today another successful step toward reaching your personal goals, there is nothing to worry about. Relax. Crack open a cool one. Watch an *I Love Lucy* rerun.

Making it all work

It's great in theory, but you just don't have the discipline, right? Take another look. You can afford the calendar. You surely have half an hour to review your day and plan the next one, right? So get started. Leave room for interruptions. Promise that you will give it your best shot for one month and I think that you will be surprised. If your concern is that your friends will keep you from hewing to your schedule, give yourself some buffer time so that an impromptu, all night game of Euchre or endless gab session won't throw your schedule out for the month.

Best of all, with a schedule as neat and tight as this, odds are pretty slim that you will plum forget about a course that you signed up for and forgot to attend all year... with the exam approaching in a half and hour and ... no clue what it is all about... flunking this course will cause you to stay in school for another year and your parents will...

Relax. You are in control. Really.

6 *FISCAL FRENZY*

– tackling the cash flow challenge

As Valley Girls went, your sister did have a certain business flair, depressing as it was to admit. It was two years ago now that you packed up your VW Beetle to head off to enjoy life in a dormitory, with a pile of overdue assignments, empty cupboards and a roommate with gas. Sis had packed her gear into the red Alfa Romeo that she won in the art gallery raffle and headed to California where "people aren't dweebs". A college education was definitely for losers. Not a surprising reaction from a girl who punctuated her expressions of distaste with "eeeewwww" and her oh-so-important approval with "right on" (a protracted emphasis on the "right").

Did she ever sweat outside of aerobics class? Did dirt only mean gossip to her? Could she consider the possibility that on sale did not mean a trip aboard a yacht? But most puzzling of all, how did she get cash to develop such an affinity ***to her****?*

Her first letters describing her new business were the limit. Just the idea of ***her*** *running her own business was akin to Madonna writing a GMAT. The first Christmas following her start up, you had sent her a Crispy Crunch chocolate bar, partly to test the refrigeration and velocity capabilities of the Post Office and partly due to your severe fiscal constraints. Textbooks, tuition and rent had decimated your carefully crafted budget. That single Crispy Crunch meant missing out on your supermarket allotted quota of 6 boxes of Kraft Dinner on a 29 cent special. You had hoped that she* ***knew*** *that you could afford more than a chocolate bar, and that you had sent it as a joke.*

The Gucci watch that arrived in return was a sobering indication that sis was a success in 'The Valley'.

Tofuscicles? Who'd have thought that there could be money in her idea of frozen tofu on a stick in the shape of celebrities?. Ever since David Letterman showed up eating one of her tofu treats on his show, the concept had taken off. Cher was spotted on Rodeo drive licking a tofu likeness of herself, while Kevin Costner was considering a joint venture with your sister, based on "Dances with Wolves" where he would sponsor a line of "Wolf Sicles". Clearly the whole concept of "Selebrity Sicles" was a winner. Hollywood was hooked. The truth was all too apparent. Sis was the rage of California and you were left in school, lost somewhere between Wuthering Heights and Macroeconomics.

As your stomach growled, a plume of black smoke rose from your tape deck, stopping Bruce Springsteen in the middle of a tune. The sudden death of your stereo was punctuated by the dull thud of your mailbox flap, with the postman depositing the latest clump of bills, destined to wait helplessly for their overdue-notice-buddies atop the dusty refrigerator.

On Track Finances

For every million dollar idea out there and every Tofusicle entrepreneur, there are thousands of starving students who must carefully scrimp, save and budget to meet such lofty financial dreams as a bag of chocolate chip cookies and an extra Long Island Ice Tea at the campus pub.

Keeping your finances on track through your school years need not be an onerous task. It does require a little planning, a dash of record keeping and an ability to painfully forgo today's excesses to avoid tomorrow's mountains of student debts, which in turn make the day after's BMW's far less attainable. What could be more reasonable?

The Budget

I know. I have you cringing already. Two thirds of you folks have already flipped back to re-read "Examining the Student Body", preferring to let your financial armageddon assume the dimensions of its choosing. It will. I know, because mine did.

The INCOME section shows all possible sources of income through the school year. It might include an opening balance of savings from a summer job, expected cheques enclosed in a letter from Aunt Mabel, pay cheques from a part time job over the course of the school year, scholarships or student loans or grants from the government (We can all dream, can't we?). Put these headings down the left side and jot the corresponding amounts under the month column when they are most likely to materialize.

The EXPENSE section shows all possible places where you might spend your cabbage. For the categories shown down the left hand side, use whatever ones that you spend money on. If you are assaulted with wedding invitations, add a section called Wedding Gifts. If you would rather die than give up skiing, rough in something for lift tickets and beer. Write the whole thing up in pencil because, well, even with all of the best planning, money does have a mind of its own.

Begin by making a simple planning work sheet like the one shown next page.

SIMPLE PLANNING WORKSHEET

			SEPT.	OCT.	NOV.	DEC.
		OPENING BALANCE	$ 2,100	$ 650	$ 305	$ − 15
INCOME		PAYCHEQUE	75	75	75	75
		MOM	50	50	50	100
		GOV'T LOAN	100	100	100	100
		RICH DATES	75	0	0	0
		TRUST	150	150	150	150
		EMPTIES	15	20	25	30
		OTHER?	10	10	10	100 C'MON XMAS!
	*	TOTAL	$2575	$1055	$715	$540
EXPENSES		FOOD	$ 175	$ 150	$ 125	$ 125
		BOOZE	$ 175	200	225	200
		RENT	300	300	300	300
		TUITION	1000	—	—	—
		DATES	50	50	50	0
		BOOKS ETC.	200	25	15	10
		OTHER	25	25	15	10
	*	TOTAL	$ 1925	$ 750	$ 730	$ 645
	!!!	BAD NEWS	$ 650	$ 305	$ − 15	$ − 105 OUCH!

By setting up a column (the columns are the vertical ones, rows go sideways) for each month of the school year, you will be able to get a handle on when the cash comes in and when it goes out, thus avoiding those embarrassing moments of being caught eating cat food or re-using toilet paper during a period of temporary insolvency.

Got down all of the income and expense items for each month? Now check them all for reasonableness. Fifty bucks a month for food might be a little light. Is that twenty that you have pencilled in for entertainment and booze really going to hold out? Revised some numbers did we? Great. Now try adding up total incomes and expenses for each month and then for the whole school year? More income than expense? Beauty. All we'll have to do is make sure that the money is there when you need it. Uh oh. Expenses a little higher than income? We will need more money. There is a section for each of you...

Balancing Cash Flows

If it appears that you have more money available for the school year than you have allocated for your expenses, pinch yourself to make sure that you aren't dreaming. Check to ensure that your math is correct and that you haven't left out any expense categories.

Still with me? OK. Now try to build a running balance for each month to see if the money is there when you will need it. Take your opening balance in your account at the beginning of September and add the total income that you anticipate through the month. Now subtract your September expenses and put the result in the Cash Balance box. For October, carry forward September's Cash Balance to October's opening balance and add October's income, subtract its expenses and put the result under October's Cash Balance. Do the rest of the months.

Oops. Did you get a negative number some place? Those are the spots where you are going to run short. Can you borrow a few bucks from Aunt Mabel to make it through the these tight times? Can you pre-pay some bills during the months when you have a little extra cash, or stretch some payments until the following month? Any way of earning a little extra cash to tide you through? Make whatever adjustments you can and recalculate your cash balances. If you have access to a personal computer, you can use a spreadsheet to save you from a lot of recalculating and piles of that black crud that erasers tend to create.

Need More Money?

You are not alone! Worrying about finances can sap all the fun out of your college days. To remedy the problem, you will have to either do some judicious pruning of your expenditures or devise some crafty scheme to make some extra money.

Expenses are usually the best place to start. Take a good look at food and booze to begin with. Endless trips to junk food emporiums can really add up. A home made tuna fish sandwich requires a little extra planning, but a loaf of bread, a couple of tins of tuna and a little mayo will keep you eating all week for the price of a single lunch at the fast food outlet of your choice. Over the course of a month, saving four dollars a day, you could save a hundred bucks or more. With eight months to the school year and say, a four year program, you could save three grand just by making your own lunch. Sounds crazy, but graduating with three thousand less debt is a nice treat for anyone who has suffered the lengthy pain of paying off school debts.

Naturally, if you can save that much on lunch, imagine what you could do with just a little restraint on entertainment. Beer and liquor are usually about one quarter the cost to buy at a store than to drink in a bar. Try throwing parties rather than going to campus pubs. By saving two or three bucks a drink over the course of your schooling, you might be able to dramatically ease your cash flow problems and shave another three or four thousand in post-school debts.

There are dozens of other ways to save money while at school, following are a couple more suggestions that will help:

- Consider getting a bicycle and using it for transportation to and from school. Bikes are less than ideal in the rain, for transporting dates or moving into apartments, but with a good knapsack, they can do the trick most of the time. Save about five hundred or more per school year over buses and the like.
- Roommates vs solo accommodation. If you can handle a little extra company, you can slash your costs of accommodation

almost in half. Check for weird habits, strange hours and significant others that don't seem to have homes of their own before taking the plunge.

The other way to ease the pinch is to earn a little extra money while you are at school. There are innumerable ways of doing this and they run the gamut from the conventional to the not so conventional. Here are a few ideas:

- Comb through the awards and scholarship sections of your school calendar. Often there are scholarships that you can apply for that relate to level of need, career interests, city of birth and lord knows what all else. Often, there are a number of these awards that don't require a superior intellect. Bit of a long shot? Maybe. But it beats buying lottery tickets.
- Check out the availability of jobs tutoring courses. Apply to tutor courses that you have done well on in the past. Often these jobs pay well and in some cases involve simply marking papers of the poor sots who are still taking the course. In all, these jobs can represent excellent hourly rates.
- Consider working at a campus pub. Even students have time and money to spend at bars and waiting tables or bartending allows you to earn tips that are likely more than you would make on other part time jobs. It can also be a fun job that will give you a break from the books.
- How about a small company of your own? Building your own enterprise while at school will help you develop some business skills, earn extra money and impress the hell out of them during interviews for a 'real' job. Some easy-to-start ideas include window cleaning, house painting, odd jobs, preparing tax returns, car washes and whatever else you can make a buck at with minimal materials. If you can get a few people working for you, you may not need a 'real' job.
- The government. Ah yes. Before you launch into a lifetime of shelling out to our friends in the nation's capital, why not investigate the student grant and loan offerings that might be available to help you – the student, the very roots of our country, the hope for our future, about to bring forth the innovations that will save us from the far too competitive nations that make better stuff cheaper than we do – make it through your humble school year as you study the classics, deftly solve complex

calculus problems and swill Tequila. Contact the office of student affairs at your school for info on what programs are out there and how to apply.

- The summer job. While a summer job isn't going to help you much during the school year, it's a good idea to do a little planning ahead for next year. When examining possibilities of different student jobs, be sure to consider the kind of money that they are paying. The highest paid students easily earn three or four times as much as their starving counterparts, allowing them to buy groceries from the regular shelves rather than the clearance sections.

Back to the Budget

Alright. So we have solved our financial worries. At least we have on paper. How do we make sure that everything goes as planned? There is a simple reason why budgets get derailed. It's easy to spend money. It's one of those relentless, ugly truths about life. Like gravity. Or entropy. Ice cream melts. The kitchen floor gets sticky. It rains on the long weekend. Money disappears.

Technically money can't actually disappear on its own. Unless you live in New York. By keeping a very close eye on it, you can ensure that your cash haemorrhages are kept to a minimum. For a month, try writing down everything that you spend over the course of a day. (OK, OK, try doing it for a week.) You will be amazed at the extra awareness that it brings to the process. You will also find that it is incredible how much you buy that you could have done without and how much less you spend when you are recording all of the gory details. Relate your expenditure records to the budget that we built at the start of this chapter to get an idea of how realistic your monthly expenditure goals are.

Happily, you won't need to record everything that you spend every day for the rest of your life. Doing it for the odd month will prove to be enlightening and will help to keep you on track. If you find that you are running behind during the course of a month, look for ways to get back on track so that the problem doesn't carry over to the following month and make you want to chuck your carefully tuned budget entirely, running up big deficits each year and kidding yourself that you will be able to pay for it all one day. By the way, if you live in North America, that last financial strategy will sound more than a little familiar.

Whatever you do, don't be a cheapskate. Look to save money on the things that you can live without. Student life just isn't the same without the odd extravagance – a bottle of Scotch, a new CD, an impromptu trip to Florida or a new pair of skis.

And on a hot day, what can beat a Tofusicle?

7 FIGHTING THE STUDENT SPREAD

– the route to a svelter you

Stumbling in from the cab, you see flashes of stairs, wallpaper and a handrail. Top of the stairs. A sharp spin to the right down the hall, into your room. Your jacket falls to the floor. Peeling off your T-shirt, you land face up on the bed. You find yourself soaking into the stillness and the blackness.

But a tightness moves in on your throat. Dryness. Your tongue tingles. Beads of sweat begin to form on your forehead, growing and joining together in a trickle. Your throat constricts further. Lights flash through the window from the street below and the room begins to spin.

Your hands grip the sheets to steady the ride. A chill rushes through your body. The spins continue. Lifting your head from the pillow makes it all worse. Your blood rushes from one end to the other like you are on an unseen roller coaster. A powerful wave of nausea grips your stomach and moves up to your throat. There is no escape.

You feel gross. Suddenly, something twists in your stomach. Too much beer. A leap from the bed and a dash down the hall. A flip of the switch and the slam of the lid upward. The dull thud as your knees hit the bathroom floor. An invisible pump finally evicts the contents of your stomach through your throat in a barrage of noise, colour and stench. Aarrrrggghhh. Another wave of last evening's indulgences blows out of your mouth in reverse order of its entrance just a few hours earlier. How did that work again in accounting class? Was it last in first out or first in first ou- Aarrrrggghhh! More delightful reminders splash into the bowl. As the tears stream from your bloodshot eyes, you rise to your feet and twirl open the sink faucets. A few splashes of your face and a solid brushing of the world's most awful tasting teeth make a world of difference.

You stumble back and sit on the edge of your bed, gazing down aimlessly at that disgusting gut that has been expanding since the start of school. In between the stresses of classes, this term has been a tapestry of beer, nachos, tequila, pizzas, residence food and hangovers. Your concentration has fallen off, your marks are down and you look like hell.

Aside from the one daily situp necessary to get out of bed, exercise is only a foggy memory.

Wait. Wasn't there a baseball game a few weeks ago? Oh yeah. It was one that you had watched on the TV at a buddy's place. Nope. No exercise. Ugh. Ugh Aarrgggghhhhh. Another convulsion, sends you sprinting down the hall...

No Choice, We Gotta Do It

Most students start off their school years with the elaborate rituals of an orientation program. Generally these programs are a lot of fun, a great way to meet the rest of your class and a recipe for exhaustion. Screeching endless choruses of school songs, parading around in sweat soaked T-shirts and consuming immense quantities of whatever is on tap, can burn out even the most diehard student party animal.

What too many students forget is that initiation period does have an ending. There will come a time when you will realise that the back to back parties will have to yield to some balance that permits graduation, marrriage and that move to the 'burbs.

One of the key components of a happy healthy lifestyle involves getting a little exercise. Ahh yes – the 'E' word. I know. Sounds like a lot of hard work. You'd rather wolf down a bag of double chocolate Oreos and watch Arsenio. Right? Well, like it or not, watching TV and eating cookies won't get you in better sh- uh, did you say Double Chocolate? Gimme that bag.

Doin' It

No choice, we gotta do it. Begin with a trip to your doctor to make sure that your new, and likely over-zealous exercise program won't cause you to blow a gasket, have your heart do back flips or free up some crud in your arteries and shut down some important function. Be sure to tell the doctor that you have seen the evils of your slothful ways and you are about to embark on a new era of healthful diet and invigorating workouts. Find out if she has any reservations or concerns with this type of approach.

Is your heart and cardiovascular system sound? Do you have any inherent problems with any of your joints or limbs? What about other problems that may be lurking in your carcass? All clear? Great. If not, follow your doctor's warning and sit on the side lines for any activities not recommended. Before heading out, ask your doctor to recommend a dietitian for some information on food and nutrition to complement your new exercise program. No doctor or dietitian? Go and see the Health Services Office at your school.

Why are we trying to get fit again? Well, fitness can help prolong your lifespan, give you additional energy, reduce the chance of injury in everyday life, reduce the severity of some illnesses, improve your capacity for sports and activities and finely chisel your physique to make everyone hot for you.

Next step is to get yourself some proper footwear and comfortable workout clothing. Shoes can be very important since the wrong ones can result in sore feet, sore knees or simply ugly shoes. Cross trainers can be a good compromise for everything except long distance running or jogging where you will want something with some extra cushioning. Find a reputable sports store to get some help in finding the right pair for your activity and your physical characteristics. And the budget.

Head down to the recreation facility on your campus. Same problem as when I told you to go to the library, right? Well, if you can't find it, trying getting a map of the campus or asking someone. Dating tip here: don't ask a member of the opposite sex where the gym is. Especially if it's half way through the school year. Also, before you ask someone for directions for the gym, make sure you have concealed your problem areas. Guys – suck in that gut, or cover it with a jacket. Girls – try that sloppy sweater look, or go for a pair of baggy sweat pants to keep those saddlebags in check.

When you do arrive at the recreation area, get some brochures to learn about the facilities that they have installed. Usually, for a small extra fee, you will be able to join the recreation complex and take advantage of all of the facilities. Note their hours of operation so that you can plan your workouts around your class schedule. You will need to work on a number of different areas of fitness, so with all of the literature of the recreation area in hand, it's time to build your fitness plan.

The Elements of Fitness

Strength

We often make the mistake of confusing strength and fitness. Strength is an important component of fitness, but it is by no means the complete picture. A brick wall may possess immense strength, but it would have considerable difficulty keeping up with you on even a lethargic day. Strength is determined by the ability of a muscle to contract against a load. The more powerful the contraction, the greater the capability of the muscle to move the load. Strength can be increased through the overload principle – repeatedly working a muscle beyond its capacity will cause it to strengthen. No pain, no gain, but take it easy for the first month to avoid injuries and always include solid warmup, stretch and cool down elements to your program.

Flexibility

Ever see one of those Neanderthal types circling around the beach holding their arms out from their sides? What gives? Sunburnt arm pits? Could be. The other possibility is that through very intense strength and size workouts, these lugs have greatly increased their strength, but lowered their flexibility to the point where their arms can't get back to their factory-installed locations. Ah, no flexibility routines in their workouts. In actual fact, the blockheads that you see circling around on the beach are probably just imitating other muscle heads who really didn't workout properly. Life remains a complex business.

To improve flexibility, gently stretch your major muscle groups to gradually lengthen them, giving you freedom of movement and relief from stiffness.

Cardiovascular fitness

Ever notice the people on those margarine commercials, outside in the sunshine, gardening, jogging and cycling? How come no one is out of breath? They didn't get that way from eating margarine. Even the best margarine.

Same story on those beer commercials. While a cooler full of beer may help to get the party started around your beach blanket, it won't get you to the Frisbee any faster.

Most of us probably wouldn't last through 30 seconds of beer-commercial-level-activity. We would start out playing a little beach volley ball and by the 20 second mark, collapse face down, huffin', puffin' and spitting out tiny grains of sand while the bronzed bikini clad babes and the TOP GUN inspired guys finished up the match. Cardiovascular fitness is the overall efficiency of the heart and the lungs as well as the myriad of plumbing that distributes all of the little goodies throughout your body.

Here's the key: by getting in at least three good workouts of twenty minutes or more each week that elevate your heart rate, you will be able to improve your whole system.

Body Composition

If you have been taping packages of hot dogs to your stomach to get that 'washboard look' this is the section for you. Body composition deals with the relative percentage of fat in your body. Like everything else, keeping your percentage of body fat to a reasonable level is a big job. It also gets a little tougher each year. Expensive gyms are capable of actually measuring your percentage of body fat, but as students we will have to resort to less expensive means.

Try a full length mirror. Guys – start with the profile view. Carrying a bit of a paunch? How about the head-on view – are those little love handles we see around that waist? OK you girls. Stop laughing and get in front of that mirror. Oops. Heading out to the Sierra Nevada to meet Clint Eastwood? No? Well then, you won't be needing those saddlebags. (You also won't need the haggard looking stogie or the squinty eyes).

Try lifting an arm and putting one hand near your head. Give it a bit of a shake. Does the back of your arm jiggle just like your grade three teacher's did when she wore one of those sleeveless dresses and wrote something near the top of the chalk board? You get the picture. By stepping up some exercise and eating less junk food, we can firm up all of those nasty excesses.

Building the Plan

Begin by figuring out which activities you think that you might enjoy doing. For strength you will have to rely on some weight training, for flexibility you will need to do some stretching, but to improve your body composition and to heighten your cardiovascular fitness, you can do anything that will get you breathing hard. The answer to that smirk and question that you just had is yes, provided that you can regularly do it for twenty minutes at a time, three times a week. Ideally, you should combine several cardiovascular activities to give you some variety and to work some different muscle groups.

Beginning with cardiovascular exercise, some choices include: swimming, running, jogging, fast walking, aerobics classes, tennis, squash, badminton, bicycling, rowing, touch football, soccer, basketball, hiking or cross country skiing. The best of these involve a continuous effort and ideally, do not put excessive stress on your joints. Picking activities that are competitive will generally take your mind off the exertion and will result in a program that is more fun and easier to stick with.

A good cardiovascular program might include a run on Monday evenings before the NFL games come on, a half hour swim Wednesday before Physics class, a regular lunch hour squash game with Cindy on Thursdays and a pick up game of touch football with the gang on Sunday afternoon. Each of the events in the sample is good for improving cardiovascular fitness, provided you keep the activity sustained throughout the period.

In each cardiovascular workout, you will want to get your heart rate up to about 150 to 180 beats per minute. That equates to 25 to 30 beats in 10 seconds. To take your pulse, place your index and middle fingers of your right hand on the outer edge of the 'Adam's Apple' on your throat, or try your inner wrist. Feel around and you should feel a pulsing at your fingertips. Try doing some exercise then note how it picks up the pace. Get used to what a rate of 150 to 180 beats per minute feels like so that you won't have to sink to the bottom of the pool or interrupt a basketball game to check it out.

Warm Up

Prior to doing vigorous activities like the cardiovascular ones above, spend five minutes or so doing some large body movements to get all of the juices flowing in the joints. Trying some jogging on the spot, some large swirling movements of the arms and some gentle bending of the spine.

With the juices flowing and the muscles lightly warmed up, it's time to get in some stretching. With all stretches, the key is to do them slowly without jerking or straining. Begin the stretch and move the limb to the point where it just begins to meet with some resistance. Hold it there for ten seconds and then try to stretch it just a little further for another ten seconds. Release and move on to the next stretch.

Stretches

Neck

Try arching the head to work in a stretch to one side, laying your head first on one shoulder and then the other. Finish up by holding your shoulders firm and then turning your head all the way to the left, hold and then to the right. Do not roll the head in a circle or you will hear all manner of crunching noises as you lay the foundation for an 'Igor-like' posture in your later years.

Arms

Stand with your one arm perpendicular to your torso and your body facing a wall. Press the whole length of the extended arm against the wall and rotate your body away, stretching the area where your arm joins in to your chest. Hold, and then try the other arm.

Use one arm to hold the opposite elbow and pull the other arm straight across the chest until you feel the pull in your upper arm. Hold. Do the other side.

Touch your right hand to the back of your neck. Grab your right elbow with your left hand and pull it down toward the other shoulder. Hold and enjoy the burn. Do the other side. This one's great to break tense sessions at your desk, too.

Backs

Backs are so controversial that I won't even tell you how to stretch your back for fear of lawsuits, mountains of letters from physical therapists and doctors and scores of paralyzed readers in traction. Ask your doctor or a qualified attendant at the gym to give you some stretches for your back.

Legs

Front of thighs

Lift your right heel up towards your buttocks. Grab your right foot with your left hand, pulling it up and away from your back. Keep about a foot of space between your foot and your buttocks. Hold. Oh yeah. Don't forget to keep your balance. (Or hold on to a chair). Do the other side.

Back of thighs (hamstrings)

If you don't stretch anything else, be sure to stretch these little babies. Pulled hamstrings are very common, painful and slow to heal. To stretch 'em without hurting anything else, lay on your back, raise your right leg and grab your leg with both hands, just behind the knee. Slowly straighten your right leg by maintaining your grip and raising your right foot. Hold. Try to raise the straightened leg a little further. Hold. Do the other side.

Front of Calves

Standing straight, cross your right foot over your left, pointing your toes so that your right toe is touching the ground near the outside of your left heel. By bending your left knee you will be able to push on the back of your right calf, stretching the muscle along the front of your right shin. Hold. Do the other side.

Back of Calves
Stand facing a wall. Lean forward and place your palms against the wall with your feet on the floor. Make small steps backward and press your feet flat against the floor until you feel a stretch along the back of your calves. Hold.

Strength Exercises

Improving muscular strength is important for both men and women. Strength exercises are best done in a properly equipped gym. Most schools have excellent strength training facilities available right on campus. I will outline a few of the basic strength exercises using weights to build and tone the major muscle groups. Before plunging into these strength exercises, be sure to do the warm up and stretch moves. If you are unfamiliar with how to adjust the weights or how to use the specific apparatus in the gym, ask one of the staff for some assistance. Always begin with a light load that you can comfortably manage before working up, especially on your first trip to the gym.

In all weight exercises move smoothly and slowly using only the muscle being exercised, exhaling as you exert yourself and inhaling as you return to the starting position. If, for whatever reason, you prefer to exercise without using weights, we will look at some other exercises that will perform a similar role without the use of weights.

There are dozens of different exercises that you can do to build strength with or without weights. I will outline a few of the simpler ones that will get you started. Always begin your new program with a weight that you are comfortable with, gradually building to a more intense workout with heavier weights and more repetitions over time. Generally, aim for a weight with which you can comfortably perform ten repetitions. Each group of repetitions is called a set. Take thirty to sixty second breaks between sets to give your muscles a chance to re-group and then hit 'em with another set or two.

The Bench Press

This is a good general strength exercise that will build strength in the upper chest and the back of the upper arms. Lie on your back on the bench press apparatus. The weight bar should be directly above your shoulders for balance. Press the weight away from your chest until your arms are fully extended and then lower the weight back down to your chest. Repeat ten times, rest for sixty seconds and then do another 10 repetitions.

To work the same muscles without weights, try doing push ups. Keep your back straight and your arms shoulder width apart. Lower yourself until your nose touches the ground and then push up until your arms are extended. To work your chest more, try a moving your arms further apart. To build your arms try doing some with your thumbs touching.

The Arm Curl

If you crave a set of biceps like Arnold's this is the exercise for you. Beginning with your arms at your side and the weights in your hands, exhale as you raise your forearms, keeping everything else perfectly still. Don't jerk your back. Continue moving very slowly and deliberately for ten repetitions. Rest for sixty seconds and do ten more.

Without weights, you can do chin ups, if your gym has a chinning bar. Try working with an underhand grip and work your way up to two or three set of ten. For variety and to work different muscles, try overhand grips and wider grip.

The Situp

Long the staple of choleric, stern-faced grade ten gym teachers, situps carry a negative stigma. Like artichokes and escargot, situps are definitely an acquired taste. Give them time and your best effort and they will reward you with a powerful washboard worthy of your suntan oil. Neglect your situps and you will invite poor posture, back pain and a flaccid gut that will congregate in heaving rolls of pink flesh.

To work the upper 'abs', try lying on your back with knees bent, your hands touching your ears and your elbows out. Focus on using your stomach muscles to raise your chin to the ceiling or as close as you can get it. Feel the burn? Love it. Hold it at the top for half a second, then ease back down, inhaling as you go. Don't hold your breath.

How many should you do? I don't know. You can do more than you think. Go easy for the first month or so to get your body used to the whole thing. Then do enough so that you definately feel it.

When you reach a point where you begin to communicate with Your Maker under your breath, squeeze out about five more. Relax for a few seconds, then get in another set. Stomach doesn't look much different after two weeks? Be patient. Rome wasn't built in a day and it has taken you your whole life to cultivate that professional looking beer gut. Give it a chance.

Now, for the lower abs. This one is especially important for the ladies. Jeans getting a little tight? Lay off the Pop Tarts and the crackers for a while as you terrorize your stomach into submission. Lie on your back and lift your legs so that they are pointing straight up. Bend your knees slightly and kick your legs up and back toward your head so that your lower back lifts off the floor. Bend the knees slightly and then kick your legs out so that they are at a forty five degree angle to the floor. Bend your knees and kick backwards again. Feel it burn on the lower stomach muscles? Great. Arrive at that terrible point of misery where everything seizes up. Sneak in five more. Enjoy.

Leg Exercises

There are a host of different exercises that you can do, but if you have built yourself a good cardiovascular program with workouts that involve leg muscles such as running, swimming or cycling, you will probably get in all of the leg strengthening that you will need. If you do want to use some weights on your legs, get some instruction from the gym supervisor so that you don't damage your knees.

Finishing Your Work Out

Take time to do some final stretches to cool down and then head for the shower. If you don't finish off with some stretching, you are likely to be stiff for the next few days. If your facility has a steam room or a sauna, even better. Get in five minutes worth, shower and get changed.

Summary

Fitness is a must to feel and look your best. Keeping a regular program of fitness going takes incredible mental toughness. It's worth it. Build a plan that you can live with, by incorporating activities that you enjoy. No one has the mental stamina to ride a stationary bike for twenty minutes at a time over a span of forty years.

If nothing else, get in some good cardiovascular exercise on a regular basis. It will give you additional energy and keep you feeling refreshed. It will also help you to build a great habit that may even keep you off the operating table in your later years.

Good luck!

8 THE TAMING OF THE VERB
– essays made easy

A month had passed since the Macbeth essay was due for your English Literature class. While you were confident in your work at the time, surprisingly, some doubts had begun to cloud your mind. The tack that you had taken was unconventional, to say the least, but then your work usually was, well different.

Bathed in the unflattering glare of the thirty year old fluorescent fixtures, your class shuffles in to the lecture hall. You saunter in, carefully maintaining your usual look of confidence blended with a studied coolness, deftly flick back your hair and come to rest on your seat. While others may appear nonplussed, you know that they all silently recognize you as the star of English 102.

How many times before had the professor marvelled at your stunning prose, your sleuth-like ability to discover hidden Jungian symbolism, your rapier-like wit and your sixth sense at unveiling layers of human emotion and drama so painstakingly laid down by the great writers of the ages past? Even you yourself had often wondered how you came to be so gifted.

The professor strode to the front of the immense lecture hall, a study in tweeds, oxford cloths, bow tie and brogues. Do they all shop from the same catalogue? There was a moment or two of fumbling in a briefcase that may, from its looks, have once belonged to Winston Churchill. Retrieving his papers, (but without another glance at them), he squared back his shoulders, and his ruddy face took on one of those thoughtful looks, usually reserved for sniffing orchids or selling bibles door to door.

He began slowly. "Greatness is difficult to define. In every generation, people seek to express themselves in ways not yet mastered by the previous ages. Some take to poetry, some to the visual arts, others to the strains of the violin, the rage and rhapsody of the piano or the lilting softness of the flute. Still others", he added, lifting Your essay, "turn their attentions to the writing of essays in a fashion so–"

Suddenly, a sharp unfamiliar voice intruded:

"That's a book, not a pillow. Library closes in ten minutes."

Huh. The professor, the class, my essay, library, brilliance, closed, oh my God. Watch – 4:50 PM Sunday. The fifteenth tomorrow and the paper will be due. A virtual bunker of books on Shakespeare's Macbeth with little accomplished except a three hour snooze. It is going to be a long night.

Organizing Your Thoughts

Before leaping in to write an essay, take time to plan it out. You have likely been given a guideline of how long the essay should be, expressed as a number of words or pages. Typewritten work should run about ten words per line and twenty five lines per page, giving about two hundred and fifty words per page double spaced, which is how you should be handing it in anyway. Read the assignment carefully to understand exactly what is required in the essay and not only how long it should be.

Next step is to make a list of the major topics that you will want to cover. Let's say that you wanted to write a three thousand word essay on baboons. That would be about twelve double spaced, typewritten pages. Through either the details of the assignment or a little common sense, there are probably five major topics that we might want to cover – Life Cycle, Eating Habits, Troop Behaviour, Home Life and Extinction Dangers. Naturally, you will need an introduction and a conclusion and whatever else your professor has insisted on. If you are working on a word processor or a computer, it is best to build your outline right on your system as follows:

1. Introduction
2. Life Cycle
3. Eating Habits
4. Troop Behaviour
5. Home Life
6. Extinction Dangers
7. Conclusion

Next step is to further break down your topics into simpler sub-topics through the use of appropriate subheadings. Again, use a touch of imagination. Life Cycle is going to include all the steps of any animal's life cycle. While you may not know all the details yet, you can likely make some reasonable assumptions. Add in your sub headings in appropriate groupings and you have built a reasonable outline of what you will need to research and write about. Here is a sample:

1. Introduction

2. Life Cycle
    a. Infants
    b. Young Adults
    c. Adults
    d. Mating
    e. Pregnancy
    f. Birth

3. Eating Habits
    a. Consumption Levels
    b. Main Food Groups
    c. Seasonal Differences

4. Troop Behaviour
    a. Bonding
    b. Fighting
    c. Leadership
    d. Mate pairing
    e. Troop Migration

5. Home Life
    a. Shelter
    b. Seasonal Adaptation
    c. Caring for Young
    d. Daily Patterns

6. Extinction Dangers
    a. Poachers
    b. Environment Risks

7. Conclusion

Compare your outline with what was requested in the assignment. If it looks like it fits the bill, you are all set. If not, modify your outline to include all the topics that you should be covering. You may also need to modify your outline as you commence your research.

Now, with twelve double spaced pages to write and five major topics, you can allocate about two pages per topic, plus one page for an introduction and one for conclusions. If each topic averages four sub points, you can allow about one half page for each. The good news is that half a page in the world of double spaced typing is really only a paragraph.

It is far easier to think of your essay as a collection of paragraphs than as a three thousand word ordeal.

Filling In the Blanks

At last. Time to print off your outline and head to the library armed with writing utensils, a pad of paper and a tuna sandwich. At the library, you will find all of the information that you need to assemble your twenty paragraphs and get this essay out of your life. All you have to do now is locate the information, get some notes down in point form and pull it all together. This neglects the small problem that you have likely never set foot in a library before. Since the library is an important ally, I will devote a section to it.

The Library

While these buildings are a lot less fun than campus pubs, there will be times when you will actually have to venture into one. Even cool types like you can make occasional use of libraries without destroying – perhaps even enhancing – your image.

To begin, check some of your orientation materials to find a map that will show you how to get to the library. If necessary, take the little map along with you as you go. The library is likely to be a large and imposing structure beckoning you to the rewards of higher learning. There will likely be an inscription to that effect somewhere in the foyer. In the front of the structure there will be a number of large heavy doors. Pull one open and step inside. Ahh. Lots of books and people eating potato chips as quietly as possible.

How on earth are you going to find your baboon books? There must be a million books in there. There are computers and things to help you, but lets not kid ourselves. Nobody really knows how to use the damn things and the few that do aren't talking. Some computer firm probably got a tax break by donating them. The book that you want probably won't be on the computer and they generally change the floors and racks around every few months just to keep it really interesting. Only the uninitiated or the exceptionally well trained would actually head out looking for a book on their own.

To make life easier, locate one of the librarians. Usually in their thirties, they can be recognized by their turtlenecks, earth-tone corduroy pants and sensible shoes. Sandals with socks are also popular. Female librarians may favour pony tails or frizzy auburn hair. Male librarians may favour pony tails or frizzy auburn hair, often adding beards to distinguish them from the female librarians. Naturally, coke bottle-glasses are de rigueur.

Pick out the librarian of your choice, avoiding any that appear exceptionally busy or those with scowls on their faces. Begin your approach as unassumingly as possible. Try some soft-shoe lines like "Gosh, the library is so big, perhaps you can help me...". Salting in words like "gosh" and "gee whiz" will help them relate better to you and if you display sufficient gratitude, they will lead you right to the texts you are looking for. They always get their book.

They may, however, get fed up with you not looking for your own books. You will either have to rotate librarians or learn to use one of those menacing computers.

With the books that you need, head off to some quiet nook and begin gathering the information that you require. If your professor requires you to cite references for your work, then begin by writing down the book title, author's name, date of publication and the publishing company at the top of a page It may come in handy to note page numbers of anything worth a straight quote.

Scan the table of contents of the book to get a general feel of what it is all about. Flip to the sections most closely relating to your prepared outline. Make notes in point form and jot the page reference down beside each note. Where laws allow, you may want to make photocopies of lengthy passages to review the material in more depth at home. In large print beside each point, write the section of your outline that the point relates to. Continue through all of your books until you are done.

Remember not to read each book from cover to cover. Look for the outline of *their* book to find just the information that you need. Rather than reading the whole book, make heavy use of the table of contents in the front and the index in the back to find just the information that you require. By scanning and getting down just the main points, you should be done the library phase in two to three hours. Gather up all of your notes and head back to your word processor or your trusty pen and paper.

Pulling it Together

I am not a big believer in numerous rough drafts. If you have built a good outline and have done your research, you should be able to fill in your outline using the information from your notes to form a fairly solid first draft. You can then go back and tune it up a bit.

Start with whatever section that you are most interested in. If any. Move down to the appropriate section in your outline and insert some room under a subheading. Each subheading should be one or two paragraphs. Re-read your notes on this sub-heading and digest it all in your mind. Are there one or two main themes?

What is a paragraph?

Get down your thoughts and those of your references, with just one major thought per paragraph. Each paragraph should begin with an introductory sentence outlining the major thought of that paragraph. The next sentence or two should provide additional information that elaborates on the opening sentence. The final sentence should provide some sort of conclusion to the paragraph and provide a link to the next paragraph.

Work your way around the outline, filling in paragraphs with ideas from your references and work in your own ideas if you are allowed or encouraged to do so by your professor. When you have filled in all of the blank sections, pull out the original assignment from the professor and highlight her expectations of what information was to be included in the essay. Are you missing anything important? Go back and dense that section up a bit. Everything seem to be there? Great. Now its time to iron out the punctuation, grammar and spelling problems that are sure to be there. This is an excellent time to get some use out of that dictionary that has been gathering dust in the corner of your room.

Punctuation, Grammar and Spelling

Ugh. If you were born after 1960, you were educated in a period when reading, 'riting and 'rithmetic took a back seat to learning whatever it was that seemed more important to the teachers of the time. Improving grammar and spelling is not a lot of fun, but it is important. Mistakes in this area can cost a lot of marks. More importantly still, it makes good sense to sort out your writing problems now, before they cost you more than marks in the business world. Luckily, common mistakes are relatively easy to pin down and correct.

Common Mistake Number 1: Using different tenses

Tenses tell when things happened. Generally in an essay, you should try to keep it all in one tense – generally the present tense, unless the paper is about a historical event. Mixed tenses confuse the reader. As an example: "Baboons stood about four feet tall and they have thick brown fur over their bodies." The sentence begins in past tense and ends in present tense. To correct this sentence, stood could be changed to stand or have could be changed to had, depending on the tense used in the rest of that paragraph.

Common Mistake Number 2: Writing in the first person

Huh? The first person? What am I talking about? The first person is a term that simply means you, the writer. Most essays should be written in the third person, or in an impersonal form that leaves the author out of his own work. For example "In conclusion, I think that baboons face extinction in the coming decade", involves the author in the text of the writing. Leave out the "I's" and the "I thinks" and keep the writing impersonal, unless otherwise instructed in the assignment.

Common Mistake Number 3: Word Repetition

Try not to use the same word more than once in a sentence or in adjacent sentences. It is not technically a grammar mistake, but it detracts from your otherwise fine writing style. As an example: "Baboons are fairly large creatures and their large size can frighten potential attackers." A better sentence would be: "Baboons are fairly large creatures and their considerable bulk can frighten potential attackers". If you find yourself caught with a lot of word repetition, get a copy of *Roget's Thesaurus* and use it to help find the word you need.

Common Mistake Number 4: Sound-alike words

There is no easy fix to this one, but a common mistake is to use words that sound exactly like or close to the actual word that you want. Best bet is to get the resident class brain to proof read your essay and then try to learn from the changes that she made. Examples of sound-alike words include: their and there, its and it's, apprised and appraised, practice and practise, insure and ensure, principle and principal, affect and effect etc. If in doubt on any of them, look up their exact meaning in your dictionary.

Common Mistake Number 5: Possessive forms

I know, more writer's jargon. Occupational hazard. Possessives are simply when someone owns something. For example: "The baboon's claws...".

In this case the possessive form was correctly implemented. If the being that owns something is singular, the correct form is "s". If there are more than one of the being (not the object being possessed), the correct form is "s". For example "The baboons' home..." would be correct if the home belonged to a number of baboons. The form "s" is also correct if the being that owns something has a name or title that ends in an "s". For example, it is "Gus' pizza", not "Gus's Pizza".

If that isn't confusing enough, consider the word its. "Its" is actually the possessive form, as in "Who took its dish?". It's is not the possessive form, it simply is the short form of "it is". In summary, check your possessive forms carefully.

Common Mistake Number 6: Typographical errors

I grow ever more obtuse. 'Typos' are simply typing errors. Often they involve transposing letters to give you words like "teh" rather than "the","otfen" instead of "often" or "ohme" rather than "home". If your word processor has a spell checker, you can quickly catch most of these types of mistakes. If not, you will have to give it a very careful proof reading. Having a friend proof your work is generally a good idea since they will be more likely to catch your errors.

Common Mistake Number 7: Run-on sentences

The issue is not how long the sentence is, rather it is how many thoughts are in it. A sentence must have one complete thought, not twelve. Read your sentences carefully. If they seem awkward or if you need to hyper-ventilate before reading them aloud, it may be time to do some judicious pruning. If it is possible to split a sentence in two, it is probably a good idea.

Example: "A large male baboon approached the troop leader, bared his chest and shrieked so loudly that it could be heard for miles around, summoning other members to step forward, anxious to protect their peers and all that they had worked so hard to build in this vast arid land".

This could be re-written to read more clearly: "A large male baboon approached the troop leader, bared his chest and shrieked loudly. Baboons responded and stepped forward, anxious to protect their peers and all that they had worked so hard for."

Common Mistake Number 8: Sentences that aren't
A close cousin to the run on sentence is a sentence that is missing one or more of the things that make it a sentence. Go ahead – help a sentence to be itself. Example "The largest baboon troop ever". This is not a sentence because there is no verb and no object. More simply put, there is no action word and no receiver of the action. To make it into a sentence, it needs the rest of the complete thought. For example, "The largest baboon troop ever, thundered along the plains, in search of greener pastures".

For emphasis or style, non sentences are sometimes used, but this procedure is not advisable for serious essays.

Common Mistake Number 9: Un-parallel construction
Parallel construction is simply when more than one item acts as the object in a sentence. The trick is to use similar wording around both objects. For example "The baboon shrieked loudly, sending the aggressors to the hills and trees." The correct form would be "The baboon shrieked loudly, sending the aggressors to the hills and to the trees". Note how the hills and the trees receive similar treatment.

Common mistake Number 10: Punctuation
Here are the most common offenders: When writing out a list of items, separate the items with commas except for the last two items, which should be separated with an "and" and no commas. A colon (:) is used to preface an example or a list. All sentences begin with a capital letter and end with a period. Days of the week and months of the year, people's names and titles, country and city names and product names are capitalized, virtually everything else isn't. When using apostrophes, use them where the letters are missing. For example, "isn't" is a contraction of "is not". The apostrophe goes where the letter (the "o") is missing, not where the space between

the words is missing. Hey, I don't make the rules, I just try to tell you how it is. OK?

The Finishing Touches: Introduction, Conclusion and Bibliography

Introduction

With the body of your text written, you are ready to add the finishing touches. Write a brief introduction that scopes out your paper and defines what it is that you hoped to accomplish. By writing the introduction last you will have the body of the essay clearly in your mind and can clearly define the scope of your work. As with the rest of your essay, keep it impersonal. Use "It is difficult to fully define the lifestyle of the baboon...", rather than "I will cover only the main areas of baboon lifestyle...".

Conclusion

Your conclusion section should be brief but should pull together the most important points of the rest of the paper. While the conclusion should not introduce additional factual information, it is an appropriate section to to add your own thoughts and solutions to the issues that you have covered. The conclusion should give your reader a neat summary of the situation and the main points covered. Suggestions for further research could be made, as well as related but differing views and directions.

Bibliography

If a bibliography is required, you have a little more work ahead of you. Begin by re-reading the assignment to find out what your professor prefers. There are many style books on footnoting and citing references. One of the simplest and most widely accepted is simply to number all references in the order of presentation in the body above, like this.[2] This is called sur-numbers. In the back of your essay devote a separate page to the bibliography and list each numbered reference in the following format: 1. Baldwin, Michael and Grizzly, William, *Baboon Mating Behaviour*, Prairie Forest: Wild Boar Press, 1989.

Also widely used is the APA system (American Psychological Association) where the author's name, date of publication and page numbers are in brackets following the quote like this:... through the forests (Brown, 1987:23).

Don't get creative in your referencing. Spend some time to understand the style required and carefully check to ensure that your references are properly quoted.

Give the essay to a friend to read over, make your final changes, print it off on decent paper, hand it in early and head off to a part of the campus that you find easier to locate than the library. You deserve it.

9 MAKING THE GRADE
– you too can pass exams

Dawn. Sunlight begins to sneak past your bed sheet curtain and the warm woolliness of your mind parts as fear rushes in. Instinctively, your head snaps backward trying to focus on the glowing red digits. 6:54 AM. Damn. You had set it for five, giving you a couple of extra hours of study time for today's calculus final. Allowing yourself only seconds to panic, you leap from your bed. The fear that began in your head has trickled down to your stomach.

The bathroom mirror highlights the corduroy bedspread marks on your face and confirms what is now obvious – you were up late studying and you have slept in. That harsh visage in front of you houses an anxious mind incapable of writing a passing exam.

Your tongue slithers over teeth wearing tiny fuzzy sweaters. You grab for the tube of… empty toothpaste. Ugh. A swoosh of the plastic curtain, a spin of the knobs and the shower splashes its icy water on you. Another unpaid gas bill?

Dried off now and clothed, you sit at your desk, desperately trying to soak up chapters fourteen through twenty three. The squiggly symbols and Greek letters of Calculus dance on the page. It is just not soaking in. If only you had looked at those earlier…

Forty minutes until the exam starts. You decide to trek up to school, to see if anyone is around to commiserate and exchange last minute tips.

The cool morning air braces your face and plays with your hair to the familiar sound of your rusty bicycle chain. Your bike follows the route it has taken a hundred times before. With a click, your machine is safely locked to the "No Bicycle Parking" sign. You bolt up the well worn concrete steps to be greeted by the throbbing masses about to write Calculus 100. Scott stops you, his face screwed up in anguish.

"Get a load of this", he stammers, "Have you tried this problem where you have to differentiate the whole surface of the moment of inertia in the place using D'Eigenvault's theorem in three dimensions?"

You have never seen anything like it in your life. The panic that had settled in your stomach ventures North to heat up your cheeks and empty your mind of any useful information that it may have previously held. Your only hope lies in the formulas that you had carefully programmed into your calculator last night.

"Calculus 100, rows 20 through 50", bellows the exam room monitor, "All papers, books and calculators off the desks."

What, no calculators? You were certain that calculators were allowed. You lower your calculator to the floor, taking with it your last shred of hope pass, graduate and enjoy an electric garage door opener in Suburbia.

The polite tinkling of pens and rulers is followed by the swooshing of fresh exam papers on to the desks. You sniff yours briefly to check for that peculiar photocopier smell reminiscent of cooked carrots. Check. You begin with what you know, carefully scribing your name and course code on the top of page one. Turning the first shaking page, you glance at the questions. Your worst suspicions are confirmed. The apocalypse unfolds.

Avoiding Exam Disaster

Attending Lectures

Avoiding the type of disaster chronicled in the previous scenario is the aim of this chapter. The key to writing solid exams is the preparation that you have been (or should have been) doing all term. The Ghost of Procrastination haunts us all.

Begin by staying awake in class. Don't spend the entire lecture copying from the board to your notes. The idea is to learn, not to improve your penmanship. By simply copying material onto your paper, you are listening passively to the material while your mind is aimlessly dusting its cerebral cortex. To listen actively, you must ask yourself questions as you listen to the concepts. Does the stuff make sense? Do the results seem reasonable? Can you apply this information to any situations that you are familiar with?

Professors have a sadistic habit of scrawling out four blackboards worth of material and then punctuating their work with a comment such as "Naturally, this portion is merely the trivial underpinnings of a far more significant piece of work which I will attend to presently...".

While you are totally lost, remember that when they say that, they mean that it is trivial for them, since they have been repeating the stuff to students for the last twenty five years. Did the Prof understand it the first time he heard it? Fat chance. He wants you to feel as dumb as he did.

Listen Actively

If you have been keeping up with your work and you are still lost, put up your hand and ask for an explanation. Don't burden the rest of the class with infinite niggling details and minutiae, just confine yourself to the one or two biggies that may be driving your crazy.

By tuning in to the concepts the first time that you hear them, you are allowing yourself at least one exposure to the material. By asking yourself questions and relating the material to things that you are familiar with, you will be *listening actively* and you will be helping to motivate yourself to learn the next piece of information.

Review

The second opportunity to learn comes during a periodic review of the material. This is best done at the end of each day, after classes are over. It needn't take up the entire evening, but aim for at least fifteen minutes of review for each hour of lecture material. The review period will allow the concepts to gel in your head and also give you an opportunity to find errors in the class notes and work through the sample lecture problems or case studies. With minimal effort, you have now seen the course material at least twice. You will also ensure that your class notes are complete and that there existed at least one point in time where you understood it all.

The Textbook

Ah yes, they looked so good lined up like shiny cardboard soldiers the day you brought them home from the book store and perched them in alphabetical order on your bookshelf. Well, even though they aren't really soldiers, it is now time to get them off the shelf and exercise their little spines. Best not to leave them in their pristine state right up until the end of the term. Or until your parents come to visit, whichever comes first. Speaking of which, be sure to eliminate all other clues that you haven't been studying before the folks arrive.

The course textbook offers another way of visualizing the information because it provides several features: it may have a number of worked examples of exam-type problems or scenarios, it operates at the pace you set, it has fewer errors than your own notes and it never comments on your learning ability or tells you that the material is trivial.

Reading Actively

So, it's as simple as turning on the stereo, cracking open a beer, laying on the couch and gazing at the pages, right? Wrong. The key to learning is *reading actively*. Start by sitting at your desk to study. Working at your desk adds an element of gravity to the moment and triggers your subconscious mind to get serious. It can also help you avoid the inevitable distractions of the refrigerator, the TV, the stereo, squeezing zits, chatting with roommates, yapping on the phone, reading the newspaper, falling asleep or waxing the cat.

Arm yourself with a pad of paper and a pencil. Start by reading the objectives of the chapter or the section headings so you are at least familiar with what you are about to learn. Jot these down on your pad together with any questions that spring to mind about the topic. Try to build up some curiosity about the topic so that you are actively searching for answers as you read. What's that you say, you can't summon up any curiosity about Calculus, Greek Mythology, Meteorology or what ever it is that you are studying? Shame on you.

At any rate, *prepare to read.* Use a highlighter to draw attention to key concepts, passages or formulas. The idea is not to create a symphony of colour on the page or to minimize the area of the remaining white space. Just go over the key points. Be sure to highlight both the material itself as well as any phrases that helped you to understand the material the first time that you read it, since you will want to be certain to review those sections later. These key points are often emphasized in the book or form the opening or core sentences of each paragraph.

As you are using your left hand to highlight, your right hand should be writing down the answers to the questions that you thought up earlier as well as the most critical nuggets of information that you have managed to unearth. You left handed types may want to reverse the procedure. Some textbooks may want to continuously snap shut on you and may require the work of one hand just to hold the bloody thing open.

Save your notes in the file that you labelled for the course. These notes will prove invaluable later when working on problem solutions and while studying for exams, their brevity will really save time.

Staying Focused

You may find that you have difficulty keeping your mind tuned in. All students do. Any type of minor distraction will be transformed into an invited replacement activity. Suddenly, paying bills becomes fiercely important. Is that a dust bunny over there underneath the couch? Better get to it right away. The afternoon soap operas, making a sandwich or the ubiquitous "ten minute snooze" will all serve to separate you from your work.

The way to stay focused is to size up the total amount of work and then set up a time schedule in which to do it. Like any restrictive program (including dieting and personal finance budgeting), success comes from being realistic. Promising yourself that you will read the second half of Hamlet in an afternoon is like taking an oath to never eat ice cream or chocolate again. You are destined to break the initial oath, with the whole program going to hell in a hen basket.

Prepare a fair schedule

Instead, give yourself a fair schedule, including ten minute breaks every hour. Use these breaks for a brief exercise period to help keep you alert and ready for the next hour. Try jogging on the spot, push ups, sit ups or whatever else you find invigorating. Set a reward for yourself at the end of your study session to motivate you to complete your work on time. By setting a schedule and tracking your performance, for example "I need to complete chapter 8-12 by 10 PM", you will be helping yourself to stay on track and ensure that are accomplishing your priorities. Over time, you will find that you are able to stay on track for progressively longer periods. A half an hour of studying intenselycan cover a lot of material.

Working Out Problems From the Text

By far the best way to learn any type of material is to actually work at it rather than using the book simply as protection should your head strike your desk during the initial stages of counting sheep. Whether it's Macbeth, Macalculus or Macsociology, make sure that you have a textbook or a study guide that has some worked out problems or sample essay questions that will test your knowledge of the material. It is a safe assumption that the final exam will involve something more taxing than signing an affidavit that you have indeed read the material.

Don't tell me. Let me guess. Laziness and a strong propensity to kid yourself has led you to discover either that there are answers in the back of the textbook, or that there is some kid in your class that you can call as soon as the problem solving gets a little tough. Right? Resist the temptation. In the exam room you won't have the luxury.

As a minimum, do all the questions that the professor assigns. If you have the extra time, do additional problems that have answers in the back of the book. There is no point in doing a number of problems with only the author of the book knowing whether you got the right answer. There is one other being who would know whether you got the right answer, but with all of the grief going on in the world these days, He probably doesn't have the time to check your work.

Most exams involve questions that extend the concepts that you learned during the term. Memorizing is not sufficient. If you have been solving math problems in two dimensions, the exam will extend it to three. If your course was on baboon behaviour, the exam questions will want you to extend your newly found knowledge to chimpanzee applications. Working out problems yourself and struggling with them will help you to get your mind in shape for that final exam.

Hard Work. There is no substitute.

To help you work on these problems, keep your class notes and your textbook notes handy. If you find that you learn something new while working on the problems, take a minute to add it to your notes so that when you study for the final, you have everything in one place.

Above all, remember to savour the agony of studying like the burn of exercising. It is only the remembered pain of studying that makes your graduation ceremony exciting. There is nothing like the straining effort to understand a fiendishly difficult problem, sketching out a diagram to understand it better and then weaving row after row of elegant mathematics, simplifying, reducing, massaging and then finally arriving at gasp, gasp the flip, flip, flip...Answer in the Back of the Book. Even if you were even close to being right, if you fix your work quickly enough you can lie to yourself and still claim victory. What the hell, no one was watching as you slipped in that extra step. Seize the moment. Savour the glory.

Okay. It's true. There are other feelings as satisfying. A three hundred yard, ruler straight drive on a golf course certainly measures up. Then there was the time when you finally found the nerve to approach Mary Sue in the cafeteria. As you neared her cheesecake loveliness, the fumes of violets, mousse and Soft and Dry permeated your nostrils and you stammered out something like an offer of a date. Her purring "Yes!" beat both the golf drive and matching The Answer in the Back of The Book.

Actually, she said maybe. But you told so many friends that she said yes, that you came to believe it yourself. The important thing is that ten years down the road, you will probably hate golf. Mary Sue will have moved to Topeka and married someone called Lance.

But you will always savour the fact that you got The Answer in the Back of the Book.

Studying For Exams

The best way to study for an actual exam would be to get a copy of the exam before you go in to write it. This is a risky approach. It will likely get you thrown out of school, relegated to spending the rest of your life drifting aimlessly from soup kitchen to bread line maybe ending up at a penitentiary, making big rocks into little rocks.

There are better approaches.

Try to obtain copies of old exams from previous years. While it seems almost too good to be true, it is not cheating. Most schools will make available copies of these old exams. If not, check with students who have taken the course before. Take the time to sit down and work your way through some of these old exams. you will be amazed at how well you thought that you had prepared and how poorly you will actually do writing an old exam. Treat it as though it were the real thing, allowing yourself the allotted time and working alone. When you are done, make notes of all the sections that you had difficulty with and go back to review the material in the text and in your notes. When you are done, compare your results with those of classmates who worked through the exam as well. If you can make it through two or three old exams, you are likely well on the way to being ready for the real thing.

Working in Groups

Get a study group together. The ideal size seems to be a group of three. Larger groups turn into knit and chat sessions where all the world's problems get resolved except the course material and a gavel is necessary just to keep the whole thing in order. As a side note, the term "stitch and bitch" has taken off from "knit and chat" in some circles. Use whichever you are more comfortable with. Back to the best size for the group. Two tends to be too small. It is very likely that unresolvable problems will arise that neither party can solve. Typically the third person will have the answer and will be able to keep the group moving along. This also provides a compelling reason why it is best to ensure that you are the third person and not the first or the second.

Ideally, the group will involve someone a little brighter than you and someone a little, uh, slower. The 'gifted one' will help the group understand the question. They will also make you sick. The slower member will ask just enough 'dumb questions' to ensure that you really know what you are talking about and keep all three of you guessing who the real dummy is. By the way, if after working in your group for a number of weeks, you can't figure out who the real dummy is, you are.

Always have a good shot at the material yourself before meeting with the group, bringing only those questions that you couldn't work out yourself. The group session is ideal for clarifying class notes, textbook problems and as a forum to compare the solutions that you have worked out to the old exams. It is best to have the group meet in person, since three way phone conversations discussing Plato's Republic can be somewhat onerous.

By attacking the course early, the final days before the exam can be used for an overall review. If you finish studying early, be sure to sharpen yourself up for the finals by doing some sample problems or questions a day or two before the exam. There is a definite groove that you will get into for each course and a particular mind set of how to solve the type of questions that are associated with that course. It is important to ensure that you are at the peak of that mind set when exam time arrives.

Writing Exams

OK. So you've studied, reviewed and written old exams. You have highlighted, asked questions, made notes, worked alone and in a group, always studied actively and all your friends think that you have become a total loser. You hate me for making you do all of this work.

But are you ready to write the exam? Almost.

Exam writing is an art form. To test your skills, take this simple test: You stroll into an exam room and you notice someone with a very bad cold, constantly slurping the contents of their mucus laden proboscis. A few rows to the right sits a shapely vision in a mini skirt, high heels, a gorgeous smile and twenty three sterling silver bracelets on her writing arm. Seven rows to her left sits a clean cut "surfer type" young man who is nervously shaking his right leg up and down, setting up harmonics that cause the adjacent three desks to resonate profoundly.

The question: Who should you sit beside?

Even a novice exam writer will recognize the peril of sitting beside the person with the cold since there is some danger of either catching the affliction or being sprayed with the distasteful effluent in the event of an inevitable sneeze. Ah yes, but what of the other two choices? Male students may be tempted by the possibility of family money that lurks behind the silver bracelets, while female students may fall prey to the clean cut 'surfer type'.

The correct answer is not to sit near any of them. The clinking of those bracelets, the vibrating legs and the nasal slurping all have the same effect: You won't be able to write your exam. Beware of slurpers, tinklers and leg shakers. Find yourself a quiet spot that is equipped with a four legged desk, ideally all the same length. It may sound like a nit, but the rocking back and forth of an ill carpentered desk can be a major distraction.

Get Out of Bed

While technological advancements like the modem, the personal computer and the fax machine should have made tele-exam writing possible by now, the concept unfortunately still remains the stuff of fantasies. The plain ugly truth is that you will have to poke your head out from under the blankets on exam day.

To ensure that you do get out of bed, set two or three alarm clocks. I know, I used to have a helluva time getting out of bed. If you are like me, you might want to use an old trick that I found helpful. I call it the 'hostile environment' technique. Set an alarm that is positioned clear across the room with the alarm set to its loudest possible setting. Make use of secondary and tertiary alarms set at five minute intervals scattered around the room. When the first one goes off you will leap to your feet to turn it off for fear of waking the entire household. While you are up, turn on your room lights, clear the curtains and throw open the window. Pull all the covers off the bed and throw them in the closet. Crank up the stereo full blast. You have now created a hostile environment where it is virtually impossible to sleep. The only alternative is to get out of bed.

One note on the hostile environment technique. On thinking it over, I realise that a big part of the success of the technique depends on the good Canadian climate that sends avalanches of snow through your window if you open it in January. With your blankets in the closet and nothing but your scivvies on, you will definitely be forced to get up. However, you readers who live in San Antonio may wonder what is so hostile about this system. Having spent some time in Texas, I can picture you lying in a bed with the window open, sipping a Margarita and wondering what is going to cause you to get out of bed. For you folks, I don't know what to suggest. Maybe throw a tarantula in your bed or something.

Eat

If you are smart enough or lucky enough to live with your parents, you will likely have a mother who will have a nice pot of porridge on the stove with one of those crusty scums forming over the surface, three eggs sunny side up, four strips of bacon, a couple pieces of toast, a glass of orange juice, a crab quiche and a nappy of fruit salad. If you can manage to haul that gut of yours up to campus, you will probably have plenty of food energy to make it through the exam. By the way, try visualizing that crusty scum slowly forming on the oatmeal while you are wrestling with getting out of bed. It may be all the motivation you need to get moving.

If you have a place on your own, an initial reconnaissance of your refrigerator is likely to yield three cans of Bud, one bottle of lemon juice, some onions growing shoots, green ketchup and a half can of cat food. Whatever it is that you have dwelling in there, you will need to assemble some sort of breakfast to maximize the power of your cerebellum (or whatever part of your brain it is that helps you to write your exam). Try to get in some protein (milk, eggs, peanut butter) and some carbohydrates (toast, cereal, jam). Don't go crazy on the coffee, too much will have you floating over the exam room, shaking with the jitters or needing to find a washroom at a critical juncture.

If the exam is more than a couple of hours, its not a bad idea to take a chocolate bar in with you to get some quick energy. The wrapper could also be used to hide some cheat notes, although I hear that the exam room monitors are onto that one.

Get Dressed

Unfortunately the concept of writing exams "al fresco" has not caught on in Continental North America, and clothing is likely to be mandatory where you will be writing. Give more than a cursory thought to what you will be wearing on exam day. While the Gucci number that you bought down south may be just the thing to attract potential dates, it may not be the thing to wear during exams, especially if it doesn't look good when it gets sweaty.

It is best to use a layered approach, since the heating and cooling systems in exam rooms tend to the polar or the volcanic. Begin with a cotton T-shirt and add layers of shirts or sweat shirts to suit. Those of you who live in North Moose Bladder will want extra layers while those from South Scorpion Stinger may opt for muscle shirts. Whatever havoc they attempt to wreak with the heating and the A/C, you will be ready. Simply add or remove layers to combat cold sweats, hot flashes and the like. Most schools will insist on a minimum of one layer at all times.

Go to the Washroom

Be certain to visit the washroom prior to an exam, whether you feel a need or not. More than one person has lost points on an exam due to an excessively turgid bladder, me being one of them. When it comes to checking your paper over for those last five marks or racing for a chance to drain your onions, there is no contest.

Make Your Entrance

Milling around just outside the exam room will be throngs of pulsing, quivering humanity, feeding on each others insecurity like so many lemmings heading off to sea. Don't be one of them. Avoid the group entirely lest you risk having your psyche and your confidence whipped up like a banana milkshake. Instead, arrive at school half an hour before the exam and head to a quiet corner somewhere that you can spend a few moments reading over your final set of study notes. With that done read something inspirational – an old Vince Lombardi locker room speech, a Martin Luther King address or some John Lennon lyrics. Whatever gets you psyched up and motivated. With just enough time to get to the exam room, pack up your gear and head over.

Get Organized

Hopefully you haven't already forgotten my advice on how to pick a good spot in the room. The front is better than the back since you are less likely to be distracted by others in the room. If you are in the early twenties age bracket like most college and university students, you likely have a set of overactive hormones in place and the spectre of rows of shapely men or women ahead of you (only you know which you prefer and these days one can't make any assumptions) may tap into your concentration.

Neatly organize your desk with ruler, pencils, pens, calculator and spare calculator, as required. Unclasp your watch and lay it on your desk as well.

When the exams are distributed, take a moment to ensure that all of the pages are present. Take a deep breath. Read through the entire exam. The objective here is to assure yourself that you do know how to approach the majority of the questions. Divide the total number of minutes available for the exam by the total number of marks on the paper, giving your the number of minutes that you can spend for each mark of the exam. Multiplying by the number of marks in a given question, you will know the maximum length of time that you can spend on that question. Use this marks-per-minute number to check and pace yourself throughout the exam. (Hope the math in this paragraph didn't confuse you. If it did, hopefully you are not a math major. If you are a math major, please help someone who got confused.)

Write the Exam

Begin by picking the question that you are sure that you can do. The key to exams is getting the points on the board early. Doing an easy one first will perk up your confidence and ensure that you don't get a zero overall. Most exams are set so that even a total buffoon can get some marks. Do these buffoon questions early, lest you spend most of your precious time on the far flung esoterica, with no time left for the easy stuff.

To do well, you must follow the three "R's" of exam writing. Listed in order of importance they are:

1. Read the question
2. Read the question
3. Read the question.

It may sound trite, but few things are as painful as getting no marks for a question that you were capable of completing. Often, a misread question can send you off on a wild goose chase, struggling with a fascinating problem that is much more difficult than the one provided for you on the exam. Gradually work through the questions, saving the toughest for the end.

As you write your paper, remember that at the other end, there will be a real live person who has to mark the thing. The marker has little incentive to go out of her way to understand your chicken scratch or search through the paper to find your answers. In fact, if you get the marker riled by forcing her to wade through pages of messy, mindless drivel, the effort may be abandoned long before reaching the nuggets of wisdom that you have so cleverly hidden.

Begin by starting each question at the top of a new page, with the question number written clearly in large numbers and underlined. If it is a technical course, be sure to begin with a crisp diagram and the axes labelled on your graphs. Give a running commentary of what the streams of mathy squiggles are all about to aid the marker in following your logic. If the exam involves essays, use an opening paragraph that lays out an overview or agenda to your response so the marker has some idea where you are headed. Be sure to state all of your assumptions as you go, no matter how trivial they may seem. You may want to use the back of an exam paper to sketch out your thoughts and clarify your thinking.

If the exam is of a type where the questions have a final answer, ensure that it reflects your pride as its creator. Don't skimp. Put it on a line by itself, draw a box around it and don't forget the units it is expressed in. Be sure to take a look at your answer after you write it down. Re-read the question. Does the answer look reasonable? Are the units consistent? Is there a way to use another solution method to check your answer?

When you have completed the exam, use any and all remaining time to carefully check all of your work a second time. Assume nothing. If you have lots of time left, you may be able to re-work most of the problems or spell check your essays. If not, at least check to ensure that all final answers are clearly marked and have their units in place. If it is one of those %$&!@ multiple choice exams, be sure that you have transcribed all of the answers to the little computer card that they gave you. Inhumane though it may seem ,the computer that marks these things generally shows little mercy and no emotion.

Put your name on the little devil, hand it in and leave. Regardless of how you think you did it's best to remain stoic amidst your pals. Chances are someone in your group wrote a terrible paper and your boasting will make their life miserable. If it was you who blanked out, remember, nobody wants to hear your whining. The main thing is... you are done.Go out for a beer and blow off some steam. When you get home, put all of your study notes away and savour the feeling. Oh yes. Don't forget to line up your course text next to the other ones so that they can all look like soldiers again.

Afterward

This isn't the end. It is just a transition.

The mission of finding a date and then keeping things flowing for several hours rolls into the quest of finding a spouse and keeping things interesting for many decades. The savoury delights of Le Fishstick may be greeted with very limited enthusiasm by your future gang of finicky kids. Juggling whether to pay the gas bill or the electric bill evolves to a similar decision between the mortgage payments and car leases.

And who knows. Your future lifestyle may even involve the acquisition of such forbidden assets as measuring cups, a dustpan and some sort of stand to keep your stereo off the floor.

The players and the props will change. The same fun and challenges are yours to enjoy for a lifetime. Best of luck to you.

Gord Stein

Secrets of the Successful Student

Gordon D. Stein

Hilariously written by a guy who's been there – and took notes!

- GET A COPY FOR YOURSELF
- KEEP A FEW FOR SPECIAL IMPLUSIVE GIFTS
- FOR SOMEONE WHO COULD USE THE HELP – AND THE HUMOUR
- AND HOW ABOUT BRINGING BACK MEMORIES?

ORDER NOW!

PLEASE SEND IMMEDIATELY TO:

Name ____

Address ____

City ________________ State/Prov. ________________ Zip/Code ____________

IN CANADA

Secrets of the Successful Student _____ Copies @ $14.95 = ________

_____ × $2.00 per book shipping = ________

_____ × $1.19 per book GST = ________

TOTAL PAYMENT ENCLOSED ________

OUTSIDE CANADA

Secrets of the Successful Student _____ Copies @ $14.95 = ________

_____ × $4.00 per book shipping = ________

TOTAL PAYMENT IN U.S. FUNDS ENCLOSED ________

REMEMBER

Payment must accompany order. If you are not satisfied please return books in good condition within 14 days of shipping date. We will refund your original payment or give you credit to another book!

This form may be copied.

MAIL TO:

CULTURE CONCEPTS INC.
"books for learning"™

Please allow 4 to 6 weeks for delivery

5 DARLINGBROOK CRESCENT
TORONTO, ONTARIO
M9A 3H4 CANADA